Yukon Tears and Laughter

This book is dedicated to the memory of all the special people who have touched my life over the years.

Yukon Tears and Laughter

Memories are Forever

Joyce Yardley

hancock

house

ISBN   0-88839-594-9
EAN   9780888395948

Cataloging in Publication Data

Yardley, Joyce, 1925–
Yukon tears and laughter : memories are forever / Joyce Yardley.

ISBN 0-88839-594-9

1. Yardley, Joyce, 1925–. 2. Yukon Territory—Biography.
I. Title.

FC4025.1.Y37A3 2005   971.9'103'092   C2005-905486-7

Printed in Indonesia — TK PRINTING

Editor: Nancy Miller
Production: Stefanie Eastcott, Mia Hancock

We acknowledge the financial support of the Government of Canada through the Book Publishing Industry Development Program (BPIDP) for our publishing activities.

Published simultaneously in Canada and the United States by

HANCOCK HOUSE PUBLISHERS LTD.
19313 Zero Avenue, Surrey, B.C. Canada V3S 9R9
(604) 538-1114 Fax (604) 538-2262

HANCOCK HOUSE PUBLISHERS
1431 Harrison Avenue, Blaine, WA U.S.A. 98230-5005
(604) 538-1114 Fax (604) 538-2262

Website: **www.hancockhouse.com**
Email: **sales@hancockhouse.com**

Contents

Acknowledgments   6

Foreword   7

Chapter 1   Yukon Childhood   11

Chapter 2   Teenage Years   36

Chapter 3   Fast Forward   51

Chapter 4   Yukon Vignettes   54

Chapter 5   Travels to Far-Away Places   70

Chapter 6   Second Trip to Florida   86

Chapter 7   Lara's Home 101

Chapter 8   Trip to Whitehorse 116

Chapter 9   Letters to Friends 123

Chapter 10   Trying Times 137

Chapter 11   My Experience with Drugs 149

Chapter 12   The End of an Era 153

Chapter 13   Epilogue 161

Acknowledgments

Thanks go to Hancock House Publishers for all their valuable work and efforts, and especially to David for taking on my third book. I must thank Arlene whose inspiration and enthusiasm have sustained me over the years of writing. And I especially thank my patient and loving husband of two years, who put up with being ignored for hours, looked up information for me, and resisted turning up the volume on his computer lest I become distracted while writing the story of people he has never met.

A final note, some of the names in this book have been changed to protect the privacy of the associated families.

Foreword

I was delighted when Joyce Yardley called in December, 2004, to invite me to read the manuscript of her new book, Yukon Tears and Laughter. Joyce and I met when she was working on her second book, Yukon Riverboat Days (1996), in a creative writing course that I was facilitating at the local college. Soon after the course, I had the pleasure of attending Joyce's very successful book launch, which was hosted by Thora Howell at her nationally famous Bookstore on Bastion Street. Along with her first book, Crazy Cooks and Gold Miners (1993), Ms. Yardley has created an impressive body of work that is important not only to historians, but also to anyone who is concerned with Canadian culture and with the communication of our distinct Canadian identity through literature. Yukon Tears and Laughter is an autobiographical novel written in a strange medley of genres and voices, through which the writer emerges as a uniquely Canadian chronicler of Canadian history.

Three things in this book particularly impress me. First, Ms. Yardley feels no need to define or defend her Canadian identity. She is a comfortable Canadian, referring to "our country" only when she is comparing elements and aspects of other countries to Canada. Second, Ms. Yardley is an innate feminist, who works all her life for women's rights apparently without consciousness of this fact. She does not ask for permission, nor does she need it, when it comes to the act of writing; and she is fiercely independent and self-reliant. Third, Joyce Yardley does not depend on any organized religion for her spirituality. For her, the world is a church in which she praises the creator and the creation by loving her life. Ms. Yardley shows her love of life in part by serving as a chronicler, writer of *Yukon Tears and Laughter*. It is apparent in all of the poems she loves, and in the poems she writes, that she respects the voice of the land and its history as much as she respects the voices of the people who live there. Yardley faithfully places her work into the infinite flow of writing.

Yardley's poem, "When," describes the birth of the writer. She addresses the poem to her lifelong partner, who is terminally ill. "I started writing when...you stopped talking.... / I had relied on you for too long," she laments. "I had no one else to turn to / Except me." The poet resourcefully turns inward, and finds therein a wealth of history, experience, and stories of the people and the places she has loved. The "you" in the poem becomes the reader, so that "...the words are not lost... / As long as we remember." "We" expands to become the human community, and the writer is no longer alone, because she is "heard" by her readers. In a synopsis of *Yukon Riverboat Days*, Yardley writes: "I am proud to have this opportunity of passing these fascinating memoirs on to you. They should not be allowed to die, unheard." And the voices of these Yukon pioneers will continue to be heard thanks to Joyce Yardley's carefully written chronicles.

Joyce Yardley arrives at Whitehorse safe in her mother's womb[1], with a family dressed differently from the Indian couple and their three grandchildren who occupy the train station where they disembark, and also from the boy on the dog sled who is sent to collect them. The topography of this place—harsh, austere, and overwhelming in its vastness—insists that its people respect each other's differences. Survival in this place is only possible by forming and maintaining a cohesive community.

In the microcosm of Whitehorse, Yukon, the girl grows to become a woman, a wife, a mother, a grandmother, and finally a caregiver for her ailing husband. When her partner is leaving this earth, she becomes incomplete. However, this is a daughter of the Yukon—of pioneers—and she immediately begins the task of recreating her past and its history, and successfully recreates herself in the process. The girl thus becomes an elder, a chronicler, a teller of tales from the edge of her world, from a "time warp." The ego that would have edited out personal dramas, mishaps, and blunders is not present. It is only by boldly chronicling all of her experience that Yardley is successful in recreating herself, whole.

The book begins with a tale of a little girl living in a world of wonder. She is intelligent and quick-witted, sorrowful and joyous, serious and filled with laughter—a fresh intellect exploring her world with the true pioneer spirit of a child:

Some of my greatest pleasures, though, were the canoe rides on Ice Lake. My dad would let me help paddle around the lake, and sometimes we took the "wind-up" gramophone along, so the others could hear the sound of music coming over the water. Other times it was so quiet all we could hear was the dipping sound of the paddles in the water, and the loons calling—with their many different voices. One day I climbed into the canoe to go for a ride with Charlie, when, to my surprise, he handed me a paddle, shoved the canoe out and said, "Lassie, you're old enough now to take it out alone. Away ye go now…

As she communicates her place, people and experiences to the world, the microcosm of her life becomes a macrocosm—the particular the general—and Joyce Yardley reveals an ethos of the Yukon with which all Canadians may identify. She weaves her materials in several genres with an interesting organization that at first appears random like the strange order of her dreams. Joyce Yardley has complete faith in this process. As a chronicler, she records it faithfully and without artifice. I applaud Ms. Yardley's courage, caring and persistence in continuing to explore new ways of seeing and understanding ourselves and our world.

Canadians are eager to explore their culture, and *Tears and Laughter* spices up our Canadian brew of fact, fiction, legend, tall tales and history that comprise our mythos. *Yukon Tears and Laughter* is witty, thought provoking and engaging. It is definitely worth a second read.

— ARLENE SÆUN, M.A. (English)
Nanaimo, British Columbia

1. In her synopsis of *Yukon Riverboat Days*, Yardley states that while she was writing the book, she found herself in a kind of "Time Warp." In this time warp her childhood becomes her present, and she looks back from there to the turn of the century. This vantage point made it easier for the writer to identify with the characters she was writing about. In the present book, Yardley has adopted some sort of omniscient vantage point from the time her family arrives in Whitehorse.

1

Yukon Childhood

Wild and wide are my borders,
Stern as death is my sway,
And I wait for the men who will win me,
And I will not be won in a day.
And I will not be won by weaklings,
Subtle, suave, and mild,
But by men with the hearts of Vikings,
And the simple faith of a child.

— ROBERT SERVICE

Whitehorse nestles in a valley between the Yukon River and an escarpment or high ridge, which runs the full length of the town on the west side. The airport is situated up on the ridge. In my early memories it held one small hangar and a little gravel airstrip. The town was composed of dirt roads, wooden side-walks, log cabins and clapboard houses with little paths at the back, leading to the outhouses.

The narrow-gauge railway of the White Pass and Yukon Route ran through town, closely following the contours of the river, and the train station was on the very end of what was then Main Street. On an October day in 1925, when my family arrived by train, the wooden platform surrounding it was almost empty, except for an elderly Indian couple with their three grandchildren sitting on one of the old benches outside the building. The old Indian man stoically chewed tobacco, spitting into one of the spittoons that were always in evidence around the station in those days. His wife, in her own language, loudly scolded the kids, who were wildly chasing each other around the premises making a general nuisance of themselves.

Anyone watching my family step off the train that day would never have dreamt that they were almost down to their last dollar. Jobs in Alberta had been few and far between during the depression. My father, Eric Richards, had been elated when the letter arrived from Isaac Taylor, of Taylor & Drury's department store, accepting his application for a job in Whitehorse, Yukon.

Looking for all the world like a successful businessman in his tweed suit, overcoat and fedora, my dad helped mother down from the train. She was all decked out in her best traveling clothes, even though she was pregnant with me at the time and very tired from the trip. The children followed her, two girls and two boys: Dora, was ten years old, Ted, nine, Wilda, eight, and Ray, seven. The girls wore frilly starched dresses and black patent shoes. The boys were wearing the only suits they owned. They looked like they might be on their way to Sunday school.

This scene proved to be too much for the little Indian kids in their moccasins and moose-skin jackets. Their grandmother finally got them in hand, and the giggles ceased. The kids retreated to a space behind the bench, hands clapped over their mouths, while they stared in awe at the newcomers.

During the previous twelve years, Dad moved from town to town in Alberta working at anything that was available, constantly trying to find something suitable that paid enough to keep his growing family well fed and comfortable. My father had apprenticed for a tailor in London, England, where he was born and raised. He also studied the performing arts, which was his true passion. He was traveling with a group of actors who were touring England, when he met my mother in Sussex. This was just before her family moved to Canada in 1912. He had been struck by the proverbial thunderbolt, and the next thing he knew, he was on his way to Calgary, Alberta, where they met once again. The following year they were married, and nothing would ever come between them again.

Always optimistic and cheerful, my father felt that someday soon they would find the ideal place to settle down and begin saving money for a home of their own. But it was not easy for a man of his artistic temperament to suddenly adjust to totally dif-

Eric Coke Richards (1911).

Grace and Eric Richards on their honeymoon (1912).

ferent conditions in a strange country, as well as take on the responsibilities of marriage and raising a family, all in the first few years of moving to Canada.

When my folks arrived, tired and hungry, in that strange town of approximately 300 people, they were very apprehensive. Had they made a terrible mistake? What sort of home would it be for the children, and what was in store for them now?

A tall man in a tweed cap, who had been pacing back and forth, on the platform, waiting for the train to pull in, came over and shook hands. "Welcome to Whitehorse," he said, "I'm Charlie Atherton. Mr. Taylor asked me to meet you. I'm in charge of the grocery department in the store."

Just then a dog team pulled up, and another Charlie, Isaac Taylor's oldest son, stepped off the sleigh. He introduced himself and began loading the suitcases and trunks.

"I have room for someone on top," he said, and with that he scooped Dora up and put her in the sleigh with the luggage. She was totally thrilled—her first ride with a real dog team. They were taken to their new home. To my mother's joy and amaze-

SS Thistle.

ment, when they opened the door there was a cozy warm house with a wood stove crackling and dinner all prepared and set out for them. Even the beds were made up. So, with grateful hearts they began their first day in the Yukon.

Isaac Taylor and William Drury were the owners of the Taylor & Drury general store, and Dad was hired on as manager of the dry-goods department. As it turned out Dad spent the next eighteen years of his life working with the company.

T & D serviced all the Yukon, with general stores and trading posts throughout the Territory. The main store was in Whitehorse, and others were at Pelly, Ross River, Champagne, Sheldon Lake, Teslin and Carmacks. They had been trading with the Natives since around the year 1900. Some of the posts were as far as 500 miles from any transportation, other than dog teams and bushplanes in winter months. The company would fly in supplies and take furs back out. Other posts were on the river and could be serviced by boat. The company had two of their own small paddlewheelers for that purpose.

Although my dad had found steady work, the wages he made, especially at the start, were meager. Mother remained optimistic. Not realizing how much higher their expenses were going to be, she got out the new Eaton's Christmas catalogue and began planning lovely surprises for everyone to celebrate their first Christmas in Whitehorse. The children were ecstatic with anticipation by the time the parcel was due. However, Dad had to give them the unfortunate news that, after paying the bills that month, there just wasn't enough money left to pay for the COD.

Whitehorse General Hospital.

With tears in her eyes, my mother went to the post office to have it returned. The Postmaster asked if she would wait a few minutes, then disappeared into the back room. When he came out he said, "Mrs. Richards, I've had a request from Santa Claus, asking me to defer payment of this parcel until such time as it's convenient for you. Now you take this back home and have a very Merry Christmas!" Whitehorse was like that in those days.

My first glimpse of life happened in the old Whitehorse General Hospital in 1925, just a few weeks after my mom and dad arrived in town. Eighteen years later, my own daughter, Norma, was born in the same room in the same hospital. And interestingly enough, the same nurse was in attendance at both births. She was Mrs. Jim Howatt; I've forgotten her first name. She was head nurse, or matron as they were called then, a tall woman with long auburn hair pulled back into a bun. Our two sons, Kirk and Ted, were later born in the same old General Hospital. (It was torn down shortly after that and replaced with the current one across the Yukon River.)

Just like my brothers and sisters, I attended the Lambert St. School, which went up to grade twelve. For education beyond that, students would have to travel to Vancouver or some other city. Any place south of the Yukon was (and still is) referred to as "outside." The school had three classrooms, primary, intermediate and high.

It is interesting, looking back, at things that stand out in your mind. I can actually remember our livingroom with the old rocking chair, and the way it squeaked when my Mom was putting me to sleep. I also remember my potty-training days. There came a day when I decided I was now old enough to go out by myself to the "outhouse." I managed just fine and was thinking excitedly about how proud Mommy would be when I told her. My little friend was waiting for me outside the door and, just to be really sure I had done a good job, I opened the door, bent over and said to her, "Am I clean?" Just then I felt a very sharp slap on my bare bottom, and with a shock of dismay, turned around to face my mother. She would come looking for me and saw a little fanny turned up to the sun for inspection.

"Don't you ever do that again, young lady. Shame on you, showing yourself like that!" Sorrowfully, I ran into the house, sobbing at the injustice of it all. I had tried only to please and had gotten a spanking for my trouble. In my mind the world was a cruel place just then, and even Mother was unkind.

I never liked going visiting with my mother to her friends' houses. I would sit there and try not to fidget. The afternoons would last forever, and I thought they would never get around to bringing out the cookies. When we got back home she would say, "I was so proud of you today—you were a perfect little lady. All little girls should be seen and not heard." I would have rebellious thoughts about running away when I was big enough.

When Mother said "no" she never gave a reason. It was just,

My mother Grace Richards (1942).

My father Eric Richards (1942).

"because I said so." It became increasingly easy to ignore the rules, as I thought they were not fair anyway. Looking back, I'm sure her reasons were valid, but because they were never explained, they were unimportant to me. Needless to say, I had many spankings. The undeserved ones gradually built up a wall of misunderstanding between my mother and I that lasted for years.

My relationship with my father was very different. I always liked saying my prayers at bedtime because then I could crawl up on his lap where it was safe and warm and nothing could ever hurt me. He would hold me until I finished my prayers, which could be prolonged by asking God to bless each member of the family, all my friends and sometimes the household pets as well. Then he would tell me a bedtime story, which he made up himself. Dad always smelled good, a mixture of pipe tobacco and woodsy pitch from the kindling he split every night. Mother was up early in the morning; she would touch a match to the woodstove and then start breakfast. Usually we had oatmeal, with homemade toast and jam.

I only remember Dad getting angry with me once, I can't recall just why, but the way he raised his voice and shook me by the shoulder is still very vivid. I sobbed for an hour with a broken heart. Mother's reprimands were ignored and forgotten, but Daddy's...never.

When I was four, I came down with the "red measles." Mother kept the blinds drawn in my bedroom to keep out the light, a precaution that was recommended at the time. In spite of all her efforts, my eyes were affected by the disease. My parents decided that we would have to make the trip to Vancouver, B.C., for the best medical advice. We traveled by train, then by the *Princess Norah* from Skagway, Alaska, to Vancouver, B.C.

Very often my dad and I stood out on deck, and one day, much to my delight, he reached out and caught a seagull by the legs, holding it there for a moment or two. I had never seen a seagull before. We drank "honeydew" on the boat, and to me it tasted wonderful. I remember being left with a strange red-headed woman (probably a friend of the family) in Victoria and screaming when my folks left for an evening on the town. I can't recall why I was afraid of her, but the terror was very real at the time.

My furry little toy.

I came back from that trip with my first pair of eyeglasses. I hated them. On the way home, I remember trading them with a small girl on deck for an adorable little furry rabbit. She was quite happy, and I fell in love with the toy, but our parents got together and made us swap gifts again. This brought on another flood of tears, and I considered dropping the glasses overboard. Somehow I knew, though, that this would be stepping over a dangerous line.

My sister, Wilda, always remembered the time she read the book *Black Beauty* to me. She had a very expressive voice and would put everything she had into the story. I was very sensitive to the feelings of animals, especially horses; and during a particularly cruel part of the story I burst into uncontrollable sobbing. Mother came in and gave Wilda a sound spanking for putting all that expression into the tale. For a long time after that I was referred to as the "spoiled brat."

My earliest memories of Christmas are of being held up to the candles on the tree and being allowed to blow them out. I was completely intrigued by the sparkling icicles and silver tinsel. I would never get to see the tree until Christmas morning, and always believed that Santa had come during the night and decorated it. Christmas was always a big event in our lives. The baking started weeks before in preparation for the week's events. On Christmas Eve the whole family would take turns stirring the pudding for dessert. Mother always had plenty of homemade ginger ale and root beer lined up in the "cold room," and a delicious lemon drink she made. She kept the concentrate in gallon jars, and we added water and cream of tartar to it before drinking. I would still give a right arm for that recipe, but somehow it got lost over the years.

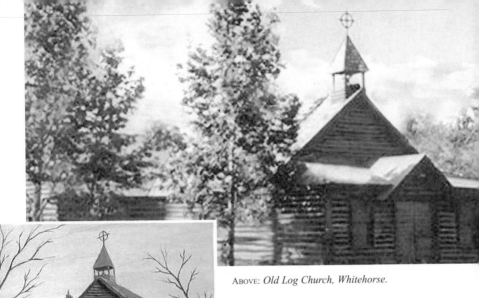

ABOVE: *Old Log Church, Whitehorse.*

LEFT: *Old Log Church, painted by the author, circa 1970.*

On Christmas morning we would open our gifts and then have a special breakfast of sausages, pancakes and maple syrup before heading off to church. I could hardly wait to get back home to play with all the new toys. In the afternoon a few friends and neighbors would drop by for a glass of wine, then it was time for the big event—turkey dinner with all the trimmings. There were always one or two extra at our table, usually bachelors or someone who would have been alone otherwise. After dinner neighbors would drop in, and adults and kids together would play parlor games. I loved those games; "the wand is passing," "charades," and "pin the tale on the donkey" were some I remember.

My parents usually went to a formal dance on New Year's Eve—a stunning-looking couple in their evening clothes. I would lie in bed, waiting for the sound of the men firing off their guns at midnight, feeling the excitement of a "New Year" beginning. It would be hard to fall asleep.

My folks were Anglican and regular churchgoers, as was generally expected of all "respectable" people back then. We attended the historical Old Log Church. With my Dad's rich baritone and my mother's rather good contralto, they were also in demand for singing in the choir. A fair amount of our life was involved in church activities, bazaars, concerts, school plays and so on. Much to my mother's embarrassment, and chagrin, my dad would inevitably fall asleep and start snoring during the sermon, and she would dig him in the ribs, shooting daggers with her eyes, while half the congregation would be reduced to giggling helplessly.

One memorable Easter Sunday, we were joined by one of our more dignified and austere matrons, who came to church with a brand new hat; a large feather sticking straight up at the back. She slid into the pew and sat just ahead of my father, who was sitting beside my girlfriend and me.

This was too much for my dad to resist. He winked at us, put his hand in his pocket, and with his thumb made as if he had a gun there, whispering, "Bang! I got that one at first shot." Trying not to giggle was sheer agony in that reverent atmosphere. Dad always had a keen sense of the ridiculous, and it would invariably surface in church. It helped make the long service bearable.

Between Church every Sunday, and Sunday school in the morning, I found myself wondering if heaven would be really worth all those hours of fun I was being forced to sacrifice. I guess the lifestyle helped to maintain our "image" in the community, which kept my mother happy, and when "Gracie" was happy so was my Dad.

I suspect what made my mother happier yet, though, was the lifestyle Dad created for us on weekends. Dad took us to picnic spots that seemed to be miles from town. Today, those places are now residential sites in the middle of Whitehorse. He took great pride in preparing barbeque pits and making picnic tables and benches from poles cut on site. We would have home-baked beans, ham and potato salad, Mom's peanut butter cookies and tea boiled in a "T-billy" over the open fire. After a strenuous day of hiking, collecting frogs and butterflies, and playing "Run Sheep Run," the kids were ravenous and returned to the camp to wolf down food and listen to the adults telling stories. Someone usually had a guitar, and we would sing around the campfire and roast marshmallows.

Looking back on it now it seems so strange, when compared to the lives our grandchildren have had, with television, competitive sports, movies, dancing lessons, skiing, mountain bikes—all these things were unheard of when my generation was growing up. We made our own entertainment and never felt we were missing anything. I think we were just as contented then as kids are now, and probably had a lot less stress.

Some weekends we would hike to Ice Lake, three miles or so out of town. We would climb the trail going up the escarpment (the old Bridle Path, it was called), walk across the airstrip and on over to the lake, with Dad carrying me piggyback part way when I got tired.

We were heading for Charlie Atherton's cabin—the man who had met my folks at the train station when they first arrived. Charlie was a bachelor, very reserved, with a small circle of close friends, which included my mother and dad. His greatest pleasure was to invite the group up to his cabin on weekends for a "Scottish" party. He played his prize collection of Schottisches and polkas, and the adults danced, played bridge and enjoyed the refreshments the ladies brought along.

Sometimes we stayed overnight, and I'll always remember eating Charlie's kippered herring and scones for breakfast out on

Joyce at 3 ½ years.

his screened-in porch on the long table he built out of poles. On the outside of the screen, he had painted a mountain scene. His hobby was making birch bark lampshades with beautiful hand-painted decorations, and hand-carved wooden chests and cabinets. (I still have a serving tray, which he gave us for a wedding gift, with birch bark and dried wildflowers under the glass top.)

As I was the only "young one" along on these weekend outings, my chore, when I got a little older, was to carry water from the natural, sparkling clear spring about a quarter-mile from his cabin. Off I would go with a gallon glass jug and my dog Pete, looking for good berry patches along the way. I picked a lot of berries in those days with my mother and her friends; we found mossberries (wonderful for pies), cranberries, blueberries, red and black currants and raspberries in season. We picked right up to the first snowfall. I remember walking through the fresh snow, our boots leaving a trail of purple footprints, as they crushed the lush ripe mossberries underfoot. At times I would reach down, brush the snow away and pop a delicious handful of them into my mouth.

Some of my greatest pleasures, though, were the canoe rides on Ice Lake. My dad would let me help paddle around the lake, and sometimes we took the wind-up gramophone along, so the others could hear the sound of music coming over the water. Other times it was so quiet all we could hear was the dipping sound of the paddles in the water and the loons calling with their many different voices.

One day I climbed into the canoe to go for a ride with Charlie, when, to my surprise, he handed me a paddle, shoved the canoe out and said, "Lassie, you're old enough now to take it out alone. Away ye go now..." What a thrill! No captain of any ship felt prouder than I did that day. The whole lake was mine alone. And although I took it out many times after that, nothing ever compared to that first day alone.

Later Dad built a cabin of our own at the lake. After that, all our weekends were spent there, with Dad puttering contentedly; whistling as he built all the endless things needed to make us a little more comfortable. He also built a sailboat, of which we were all very proud.

Ice Lake no longer exists. When the U.S Army arrived in

Mom and Dad with their grouse catch.

Whitehorse they put in a Beam Station close by and cut down all the trees around the lake. Some ice company began harvesting the ice in the winter, and eventually the little lake, and the fresh springs that fed it, all dried up.

For many years Dad, Mom and Charlie went on grouse-hunting expeditions together in the fall, and hiked on snowshoes in the wintertime.

More Memories

I remember an old phonograph player at home with a big curved horn. In the ads they showed it with a dog sitting with his head cocked to one side, listening intently to "His Master's Voice." I remember some of the records they played—and my mother being entranced by a red-headed singer called Rudy Vallee. My father enjoyed classical music and would listen to it for hours, smoking his pipe and daydreaming.

Our next-door neighbors were people by the name of Smith; they had a little girl called Linda. Linda couldn't yet speak when I first remember her. I was a couple of years older, but we played together. Our yards were adjoining, and even at the tender age of four, I felt a responsibility toward her, as Mrs. Smith was always admonishing me to watch her little girl. If Linda ever did anything wrong, Mrs. Smith would blame me and complain to my mother.

When Linda learned to talk, she would always refer to somebody called "my Dame." It took a long time before her mother finally realized that this was an imaginary friend she had invented and was fiercely devoted to. She slept with her, ate with her and blamed her for everything that went wrong.

One day Mrs. Smith left me to watch Linda, while she went to the train station to pick up some high-ranking friends, who were coming to stay a with them for a few days She had planned for weeks in order to have everything first class and spotless. Linda and I waited, running up and down the front steps until we got tired of the game. It was a very hot, dry, summer day and the heat waves were coming off the porch. Linda leaned over the railing and spat on one of the steps below. It made a lovely little "splat!" on the dry weathered surface, spreading out in an irregular circle. Next turn was mine, and I tried to spit farther than she did... Soon we were getting quite creative, and had a variety of patterns and swirls by the time Mrs. Smith arrived home with her guests. Linda went running, "Mommy, Mommy, look what we did!" she cried, proud as punch. Her mother took one look; her face got beet red.

"Go on up folks, I'll be right there," she said sweetly, and her friends went inside the house. Linda started crying.

"My Dame did it," she said. Furiously, her mother turned on me, and said, "This is all your fault. Linda would never think of anything like this. You are rude and bold and ugly!" and she shook me until my glasses fell off.

Utterly deflated, my self esteem at zero, I ran home and locked myself in my room. It must be the glasses—everyone hated me and always would. Why did I have to wear them? It just wasn't fair. I wished that I could die right then.

When my brother Ray was around ten, Mrs. Smith sent him on an errand to the store. Being a very active boy, it was always a challenge to keep him in shoes, and at the time he had a hole in the ones he was wearing, which he had stuffed with newspaper. When he returned with Mrs. Smith's groceries, she offered him twenty-five cents. Ray replied, "No, thank you, Mrs. Smith, my folks won't allow us to take money for doing favors. Glad to help out." He could see a storm brewing when the lady's face turned red, but before he could duck out, she yelled, "Well you tell your mother, poor folks like them can't afford to be proud—just look at your shoes!" We all had a good laugh over that one, later.

It seems curious that I feel compelled to include someone like Mrs. Smith in this story, but I believe that all the events in a person's formative years, whether positive or negative, help to shape one's personality. I was a very intense child, serious minded for my age, with an insecurity that I didn't outgrow for many years.

One day my mother woke up with a splitting headache and by noon was quite ill. She said, "I want you to go to the schoolhouse and get Dora, tell the teacher I'm sick and she must come home right away." My sister Dora was ten years older than I was.

Fearing something terrible might happen to my Mom, I ran as hard as I could all the way to the school. I tried to reach the doorknob, but couldn't quite make it by standing on my toes, so began pounding on the door. Finally it opened, and Miss Milne stuck her head out, "Go away, you're disturbing the class!"

"My Mom needs Dora!" I shouted. The door was closed in my face. Maybe Mommy will die, I thought, and I began pounding and kicking at the door again. She opened it once more and realized by my tears how upset I was. So Dora ran home, and I was invited into the classroom. Once inside, my feelings were soothed, by being allowed to sit in a real school desk, and color pictures. Mom was okay by the time I returned home.

The Drama Club

My father had some experience in acting with a group in England before he came to Canada in 1912. It wasn't long after moving to Whitehorse that the urge to act surfaced again, and he recruited a group of enthusiastic "would-be" actors and started up the first "Whitehorse Drama Club." Over the years they produced a series of very popular plays; with my dad being the producer, director, make-up man and set designer. As the group grew in experience, he was able to delegate some of those jobs to the others. It became a kind of status symbol to get a part in one of Dad's plays, and in a town where entertainment was limited, to say the

Mom and Dad in costume.

least, they went over with a bang. Any proceeds left over after expenses were donated to different charities. Some of the plays they put on included *Captain Applejack, A Little Bit of Fluff, What Happened to Jones, Too Many Bathrooms*, and various other vaudeville acts. I was too young to remember most of them, but I still recall the masquerades, and our family winning ribbons for "best costumes" that Dad made for us. I have old snapshots of myself and a little friend, Larry Porter, dressed as "bride and groom." and seated on a huge yellow half-moon, set against a black background with silver stars. Whitehorse was partial to masquerades when I was a child, and my father was in his element when planning for these occasions. I seem to have lost a good picture of mother taken before I was born. She was dressed in a huge and very realistic can of "Nabob Tomatoes," with her head inside a red mesh tomato. Evidently she was pregnant with me at the time, and didn't want to miss out on the fun, so Dad made the outfit for her, and off she went to the masquerade.

In his spare time Dad made extra money by painting signs, logos, etc., for local businesses. He designed the big white horse on the Whitehorse Inn, and the letterhead for the local newspaper, the *Whitehorse Star*, which they used for many years and may still be seen in the local archives.

My first marriage
(Old Log Church, Whitehorse).

Larry Porter and Joyce Richards
"on our honeymoon."

The cast in one of
Dad's plays.

The Whitehorse Star

October 1, 1926
Eric Richards is making splendid progress in training of local
talent for the production on October 8th of that popular comedy.
"A Little Bit of Fluff." This play will make even a bigger hit than
"What Happened To Jones." Indications all point to a record
attendance.

27

Annie Lake

Annie Lake was another favorite spot when we were kids. The Porter family had a cabin there, and sometimes in the summer months, Mrs. James Porter (Gertie) would invite my mother and I to come and stay with them for a few days. To get there, we had to take the White Pass narrow-gauge train from Whitehorse, twenty-two miles or so down the line. Theresa, one of the Porter girls, was around my age—a bouncy, dark-haired girl with round blue eyes. Robson was the railroad station there, and a man by the name of Charlie McConnell always met us at the train, and we would go over to his roadhouse for tea and fresh-baked cinnamon rolls. Then Theresa and I, with her sisters, Pinkie and Phyllis, would jump in the back of Charlie's old pickup, with Mom and Mrs. Porter riding in front, and away we'd go. It was ten miles over the narrow dusty road to the cabin at Annie Lake.

I remember the stairs up to the attic, where Theresa and I slept. The floor was bare wooden boards, and the cracks between them were wide enough that we could lie on our stomachs and watch what was going on downstairs when we were supposed to be sleeping. Our fathers came out from Whitehorse for the weekend to join us, and the adults played bridge in the evenings. Theresa and I stifled giggles overhead, while we listened to the usual squabbles that ensued when someone's partner trumped an ace. Jimmy Porter was a short feisty man, who used to be a bantam prizefighter in his younger years. He was known for his colorful vocabulary, and, characteristically, the air would be blue with profanity during the bridge games. What always amused my dad were the times when Jimmy would assume the role of a perfect gentleman. When an occasional 'damn,' or 'hell' slipped innocently from his lips, he would apologize, "Oh, pardon my French!" he would say.

When the card game was over Theresa and I ran downstairs in our bare feet and nightgowns, under the pretence of needing a drink of water, and wheedle our folks into giving us sandwiches to eat in bed.

There was a small pond that was formed by an underground spring close to Annie Lake, I remember. It provided us with hours of rich entertainment, as it was home to a variety of small water creatures such as frogs, minnows, water beetles, little black

Ray Richards.

leeches and something we used to call hair eels, because they were not much thicker than a hair, and they would corkscrew through the water so quickly you had to be really fast to catch them. The summer days were long, lazy and hot when we were kids. It felt so good to wade in the pond and let the cool slippery mud squish up between our toes. And it was fun to watch the water bugs scramble out of our way. We would put them in a glass jar and take them home to study for a while, until we tired of this game and looked for new adventures to embark upon.

Theresa and I tagged along with our mothers while they picked berries or took us fishing in the rowboat. The grayling fishing was unbelievably good at that time. Mom and Mrs. Porter caught as many as they wanted in a matter of minutes. They would fry them in butter, and the fish would curl up in the pan. Then we would have a competition to see who could eat the most. Sometimes we would even have them for breakfast.

One day when we were still preschool-age, Theresa and I decided to go for a walk by ourselves. We had butterfly nets and started off down the trail toward the Robson station. We were never supposed to go beyond earshot because of bears in the vicinity, but this day we were feeling adventuresome and just kept on going. We ran and played and explored, exhilarated by our newfound freedom, until our energy finally ran out. Not realizing how far it was back home, we were almost crying with fatigue, hunger and thirst when we finally got back to the cabin.

There was no sympathy forthcoming from our distraught parents, believe me! I don't think we sat in comfort for a few hours after those spankings. Later that day Charlie McConnell arrived in his truck. He had noticed little footprints on the dusty path just about half a mile from the roadhouse, and followed them to Porter's cabin to see if everything was all right. The adults couldn't believe we had walked that far, but there was no refuting the evidence that Charlie had witnessed.

Charlie McConnell also had a sawmill at Robson. A prospector himself, he had built the roadhouse there to accommodate the miners and prospectors in the vicinity. Rumor had it that the Wheaten River area looked very promising, and could become the site of a new gold rush. This never came about, but many a prospector enjoyed the warmth and hospitality of "Charlie's Place" just the same. Many years later, rich deposits of ore were discovered in the Wheaten country, but unfortunately Charlie was not around to see the resulting activity.

Wilda Richards

Ted Richards.

Brothers and Sisters

I remember more about my sister, Wilda, who was eight years my senior, than I do the other members of my family. My brother Ted was always grown-up in my mind and seemed to be away much of the time in the Mayo area. Ray was the tease in the family, and he loved to get me hopping mad. When I started pounding on him he would pick me up by my belt with one hand, and hold me out at arm's length where my flailing fists and feet weren't long enough to reach him. But he took time to play games with me too, sometimes, and I was secretly very proud of both my "big brothers."

Dora got married and went away when I was five. I remember her coming into my room and kissing me goodbye; her lips were wet with tears, which made me cry too. I didn't want her to leave to us.

One day Ted came home on one of his visits and announced that he had a special treat, which I would learn about when I came home from school. All day I tried to concentrate on my lessons without success. After the longest day of my life, I ran home as fast as my legs would carry me. What excitement when he said he was taking me to a movie! It was the first one to come to

Whitehorse, a silent movie starring Charlie Chaplin, in the old NSAA Hall (North Star Athletic Association). All the entertainment in town was held at that hall—dances, concerts and basketball games. I felt almost grown-up walking home that night with my brother.

Wilda inherited the job of babysitting me. One evening, when I was around six, and she close to fifteen, my folks went to Ice Lake for the night. Wilda and her friend, Lorraine, were stuck at home, looking after me, and just turning inside out with anxiety to go to a party that some "groovy" boys were throwing. I could appreciate how important it must have been to them when I went through the same stage, nine years later. At the time, however, I was afraid of the dark, so when they pleaded with me to stay home in bed (just for a little while!), I threatened to tell Mom on her.

"We'll give you a cigarette if you don't tell," they said. "But you can't smoke it until tomorrow." This was too much to resist, so a bargain was reached, and they went off to the party. Immediately I lit up the cigarette. I sat there coughing and coughing, consoling myself by thinking, "They finally realize I'm almost grown up now." But try as I might to convince myself later on, I couldn't sleep a wink. I lay there listening to every creak in the house, imagining spooky things in the dark. I must have finally fallen asleep, because suddenly I sat bolt upright in a cold sweat. A loud raucous shriek came from above my head somewhere, and I lay there, frozen in terror, not daring to move a hair.

It seemed as though an hour passed before I could move, and when I did I leaped into my clothes, ran out of the house (with no coat on) and headed across town to Mrs. Bruce Watson's. It was dark, and my teeth were chattering with cold and fright. Not a soul was on the streets at that hour. As I passed a fenced-in house, a little dog came running to the gate, barking fiercely. This added to my fears so greatly that I turned and ran back home. Watson's house seemed a hundred miles away right then. I went back to bed, covered up my head and sobbed myself to sleep. I thought I would die with fright, and imagined that the devil was punishing me for smoking that cigarette.

The next day I heard that same sound again. There was a big black raven cawing raucously on the roof of our house. Having survived that trauma, I toughened up considerably and contemplated blackmailing those two girls in the future, if necessary.

My sister Wilda was my role model when I was a child, and I wanted more than anything to grow up just like her. I thought she was the prettiest girl in town, and she could sweet-talk me into almost anything. She would put on funny little acts, just for my benefit, and I would giggle myself into hysterics. I guess she got her sense of humor from my Dad.

I couldn't wait to go to school. When the day finally arrived though, I was the only one wearing glasses, and the kids stared and made fun of me. They dubbed me four-eyes, and the humiliation was hard to bear. I decided to make those kids eat their words, and show them I was as smart as they were. I studied longer and tried, unsuccessfully, to outdo them all in the running races on Sports Day.

My first teacher was Miss Estelle Cameron (who was still attractive and active in when I last saw her in 1995). I printed my first composition in grade two, and it turned out quite well, I guess, because Miss Cameron enthusiastically scrawled a big red

Dora Richards

"E" for excellent right across the sheet of foolscap it was printed on. Not understanding her motive, nor what the letter stood for, I was crestfallen that she had actually scribbled on my work, and I proceeded to rub out the offending E—in the process rendering the whole composition unintelligible. When Miss Cameron asked me for it later to show Mr. Hulland, the principal, she was very annoyed that I had maliciously ruined it; not realizing, of course, that I thought she had done the same thing. A double misunderstanding, and I ended up in tears with hurt feelings and wounded pride.

Memorizing poetry and lines always came easily, and I began to get leading parts in the school plays. Pretending to be someone else in a play, I would forget my shyness, and get right into the part.

The Skating Rink

The skating rink was not only a hub of activity in the winter months, it was the main nucleus for meeting and socializing with friends on weekends. Located in the south end of town, it was an easy walking distance for everyone. There was a four-foot board fence all around it. When the snow was cleared off the ice, it was thrown over the fence. After a while the piles of snow built up and settled until they became quite hard. They served quite effectively as bleachers, and the town folks watched the hockey games from this vantage point.

The only building there was a small lumber cabin with a wooden floor and benches for putting on skates. There were spikes driven in the walls, on which to hang hockey gear, and a pot-bellied wood heater that was always red hot. On cold days people would take turns around the stove, rubbing their hands and stomping the snow from their boots or moccasins, rosy cheeked and with their breath turning to misty vapor. Between periods, the kids could get out on the ice to skate and push the puck around.

The high-packed piles of snow served another purpose. When I was around six years old, my friends and I used to dig tunnels through them and build playhouses there. Why we were allowed to do this I'll never know, surely it must have been dangerous; maybe our parents never realized we spent so many hours pursuing this fascinating game. We had, what seemed to us then, long, long tunnels with secret alcoves going off here and there with mysterious turns and twists. We brought toys; dolls to live in the crystal snow palaces; toy stoves to keep them warm and little piles of kindling. We even had spades for them to dig out their trails in case of slides.

The shadows on the walls and ceilings of our snow palaces were icy blue, but it felt warm as toast inside. If guardian angels really exist, they must have been looking out for us, because those tunnels never caved in.

2

Teenage Years

My girlfriend, Gladys Wilson, and I loved to take off on long hikes with my husky dog, Pete, at our heels. Very often we went to the Whitehorse Rapids, an area on the Yukon River, roughly two miles south of town, named by the early miners because the crest of the turbulent waves reminded them of white horses. We would walk down the railway track, then over the rotting wooden ties of the old "tram-line," a relic of the gold rush era built before the White Pass constructed the railroad in 1898.

We would continue down a narrow path to the rapids. We had to shout to hear each other over the rushing noise of the white water. If we got close enough, the cold spray would mist our faces. Even on a hot summer day, the cool, fresh air along the riverbank was exhilarating. We picked crocuses and pussy willows in the spring and spent a lot of time sitting in the grass, looking for four-leaf clovers and discussing the local boys. In the fall we would go to the rapids with my mother and her friend, to help them pick blueberries and red currants, while Dad tried his hand casting for grayling.

At the turn of the century, of course, there was lots of activity on the rapids as the miners headed for the Klondike gold fields and rafted all their supplies down the river. A good many of them turned back at this point, having lost all their supplies in the turbulent water, when their canoes overturned. In our time, though, it was a peaceful and relaxing place to spend a day. There was a large screened-in pavilion where people could take a picnic lunch and get away from the ever-present mosquitoes. A sign on the wall proclaimed it as the Robert Service Camp and many a

My best girlfriend, Gladys.

church or school picnic was held there. I remember the grounds around the camp were always kept tidy, not a gum wrapper or cigarette butt to be seen. It was easier, I guess, in those days, because there were no such things as styrofoam cups or pop cans. (I don't even remember paper towels...and certainly not plastic bags.)

The rapids disappeared with the building of a large dam for hydro purposes. A lake was formed, named Schwatka Lake, and now a cruise boat by the same name operates a short tour "up stream" a few miles for the enjoyment of tourists. There is also a fish ladder in the vicinity for the spawning salmon.

The Swimming Hole

A short walk north of town along a dirt path through the trees was the swimming hole. It was actually a secluded overflow from the Yukon River, and the water got quite warm during the summer months. Kids and grown ups alike enjoyed swimming there.

One day, when I was about nine, my sister and her friend, Lorraine Watson, took me along with them for a swim. They sat on the grass, while I went behind the canvas that was nailed to two trees, slipped into my bathing suit and waded out behind the other kids, who were already way out in the water splashing and shouting. The water felt cold, and I stood there shivering, still within earshot of Wilda and Lorraine, who were having an animated conversation about boyfriends, in all probability.

"Go on out with the others," Wilda called, "Don't be a sissy, you'll warm up once you've ducked." Reluctantly, I inched my way in, and just as I decided to duck, I stepped in a hole or drop-off, and down I went. Nobody noticed what happened, and I must have fainted, because the next thing I remember was sort of floating underwater. I could vaguely hear my sister shouting, "Joyce, Joyce!" and remember thinking, " I hope they don't find me yet." It was such a pleasant, almost euphoric, experience just floating weightlessly there in a dreamlike state of mind. No sense of panic or discomfort at all. Finally someone grabbed me by the legs and carried me to shore, where the sensation was rudely shattered. I began choking and heaving, as they pumped water from my lungs.

I'll never forget Wilda's face, telling Mom, "We almost lost her," and I have to admit I enjoyed all the extra attention and hugs I received. But I was afraid of water for a long time after that.

When Wilda was sixteen, her boyfriend was allowed to

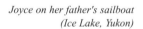

*Joyce on her father's sailboat
(Ice Lake, Yukon)*

come to the house, to pick her up for a date or to spend an evening with the family. He was very good looking, and I had a little crush on him. Usually though, he would come over after my bedtime, but I listened to them talking through a crack in the door. I would make numerous trips through the livingroom to the kitchen, for drinks of water, in my pajamas and with my hair wrapped in the white strips of rag my mother used to make ringlets. I would steal a peek at him coming and going, and thought in my heart that he really loved me more than my sister. His name was Alfie Burian.

Alfie owned a motorcycle and looked so handsome in his helmet and black leather jacket. One day they took me for a ride. Wilda rode behind him, and they put me in the sidecar. I couldn't believe anything could go that fast. After that he could do no wrong in my eyes. I intended to grow up quickly and marry him before my sister got her hooks into him. Wilda and Alfie were not contemplating marriage, however. Tragically, he was drowned a few years later, while driving a bulldozer across the Stewart River.

Swimming Lessons

When I was thirteen, my mother decided I had better learn to swim. She asked a local bachelor, who used to teach swimming for a fee, to give me lessons. The second lesson, I decided, was the last one. My swimming hadn't progressed at all, and I hated the way his breath smelled, and how he would run his hands up and down my body, when he was teaching me to float. "You have a beautiful body," he told me, but I wasn't impressed.

"Dirty old man," I thought. Embarrassed to tell my mother about this, I just told her I wasn't having any more lessons. An argument sprung up, and ended with orders for me to go back the following Saturday afternoon.

When the day came, I was up early and out of the house down to the swimming hole by myself before breakfast. I would learn to swim on my own if it killed me. I tried to stay afloat in that water, sinking again and again, and getting water in my eyes and nose. At last I began to get the hang of it, and an hour or so later, was doing a pretty fair breaststroke. What a victory that was. I went back home and announced that I could swim now! Of course, my parents had to come down with me to make sure, but they had to admit that I really didn't need any more swimming lessons.

Sex Lessons

I got my first hint of what sex was all about from Shirley. She was a grade ahead of me in school, and was one girl I couldn't outrun in the races. I always liked Shirley, although I did feel a bit intimidated by her—she was so self-assured. I wanted to be as popular and outgoing as she always seemed, but I was shy. And she didn't have to wear glasses. There was a sense of competition between us. At times, however, she and I hit it off quite well. During one of these intervals, the two of us were sitting in my yard talking about life. Shirley brought out a package of cigarettes and offered me one. I coughed and spluttered and turned red with embarrassment. Shirley nonchalantly inhaled, flicking the ash away with style, and remarked, "This is an excellent brand. I wish it were a mile long." She's so cool, I thought. The subject turned to boys and sex, and I told her, "Well, I'll never do that!"

"Oh no?" she said, "Your parents do it don't they?" I was numb with shock.

"Of course not. Don't you dare suggest a thing like that. They would never ... !"

I left her there, laughing, and ran into the house. For days I was troubled by what Shirley had told me and finally had to tell my sister about it. Wilda explained to me about the "birds and bees," and I had to make some attitude adjustments in my thinking.

Eating Out

In those early days in Whitehorse, eating out, as we know it now, was something most local residents did very seldom. There were three hotels in town, two of which served meals, and a couple of restaurants. These were frequented mostly by summer tourists from "Outside." Town people would put on dinner parties, usually followed by a game of bridge for their entertainment.

The food at the original Regina Hotel had an especially good reputation. The hotel was owned and run by Mr. and Mrs. Ole Erickson, solid salt-of-the-earth people. They were the parents of a school friend of mine, Gudrun, or Goody as we all called her. She was an attractive slim girl with delicate features, fair skin and long shiny blonde hair. Each year when her birthday came around, all the kids her age were invited to the party. We looked forward to this very much. It was a rare chance to eat in a real restaurant. We would sit in the dining room, and a waitress would serve our lunch. Mrs. Erickson would hover over us, making sure we all had plenty of food and treats. She was a hard-working woman, who always set very high standards in cleanliness and hospitality in her hotel.

Goody's hair was washed and brushed every night without fail, and if there was one wrinkle in her bedspread, the whole bed would be stripped and remade. Along with being efficient, however, both Gudron's parents were kind and thoughtful people. I remember Mr. Erickson sitting in his rocking chair in the lobby with the shiny waxed floors, smoking his pipe and watching the world go by or reading his Swedish newspaper.

The family of another school friend of mine, Evelyn (Babe) Richards, also owned a hotel, The Whitehorse Inn, which was the hub of activity, especially for the younger crowd in town. It boasted a Cabaret, where teenagers could dance to the jukebox and drink cokes.

Babe, even as a schoolgirl, used to talk about having a large family. She loved kids and would spend her recess at school knitting little things for her hope chest. Much later, her wish came true, and eventually she raised eleven very attractive children. Her father was T. C. Richards, owner of much of Whitehorse in those days, and a legend in his time.

The third hotel in town was the White Pass Hotel, and was run by a feisty little German lady, Mrs. Vioux. Its claim to fame was the rather seedy beer parlor, where the hard drinkers hung out. I guess Mrs. Vioux wasn't taking any chances, as she kept her shotgun handy.

When Halloween came around (providing there was snow on the ground), the more adventurous of us would throw snowballs at the beer parlor door. We could always depend on her to come out and chase us down the street with her shotgun. When we tired of this looked for the two policemen in town to pelt from a distance, and then we would really run, with hearts pounding, to hide. Somehow we were never caught, although they made a great show of looking for us. When most of the outhouses and woodpiles in town were knocked over, we would traipse back home, happy and exhausted.

The next day at school there was a ritual visit by the police; and the guilty ones asked to hold up their hands. Even the kids that had nothing to do with it raised their hands for this one, knowing what was in store. It meant missing a whole afternoon of school, while we were taken all over town to pile the wood again and push up the outhouses. Then we were taken to the Inn, where they would order ice cream cones for us. This was almost as much fun as the night before.

My closest girlfriend, though, was young Gladys, because she always had a sense of adventure that matched my own, and we could dream up all kinds of exciting schemes to keep occupied. Gladys married the same year I did. A U.S. Army man, Charles Hersman, took her off to Spokane, Washington, where they made their home, raised a family and lived until, tragically, she died of cancer in 1993.

Uncle Leslie Richards

My dad's brother flew up to visit us for the first time in 1940. Uncle Leslie (his own family called him "Poppy") was born in London in 1880. He fought in the Boer War for three and a half years, and moved to San Francisco soon after that. He was a shipbuilder at the Bethlehem Steel shipyards and raised his family in San Carlos, California.

Uncle Leslie arrived at the airport just bursting with enthusiasm for the flight he had experienced (his first). He thought the mountains and lakes in our north country were magnificent. He came armed with a movie camera. I had never seen one before, but by the time he left we were all very well acquainted with it. He took pictures of all my family continuously and used rolls and rolls of film on the "Fantastic!" countryside. His enthusiasm was boundless and infectious—we all fell in love with him. I had found a kindred spirit, and we were immediate pals. He bought me my first hat and a little blue butterfly-wing ring, which I treasured for years, until it went through the washing machine one day by mistake and came out all scratched. I kept it anyway.

Uncle Leslie Richards

Gladys and I went on many hikes with Uncle Leslie. We explored new trails and fished in the rapids. Years later, at ninety, he was still hiking three miles a day. He was an avid sports fan and kept right up on all current news and events until the day he died.

Before Uncle Leslie went back home to San Carlos, he took my folks aside and suggested to them that after I graduated he would like to give me the opportunity of going to University in San Francisco. He would supply the tuition fees. He thought I had a creative mind and should definitely have the advantage of a good education, which in his opinion was best obtained in the States.

However, college days seemed like eons away in the future, and just a year later fate intervened in the person of Gordon Yardley...and my plans for the future took a new and different turn.

We put Uncle Leslie on the (stupendous!) plane with tears of affection in our eyes and watched him soar homeward.

Our Theatre

There was an article in the June 11, 1937, *Whitehorse Star* referring to the opening of the new theatre.

Lovely New Theatre Draws Capacity Crowd at Opening Picture.

Patrons Loud in praise of Excellent Sound Equipment.

The town's new theatre, built by J.R. Alguire, pioneer resident and business man of Whitehorse, opened officially on Saturday night with the premiere showing of the film, "Desire," starring Gary Cooper and Marlene Dietrich, with a fine supporting cast of characters. From start to finish, the large audience was kept constantly enthralled, not only by the feature presentation, but also by the comic antics of "Popeye the Sailor," and the peppy music of Anson Weeks and his orchestra, while newsreel, parts of which showed the havoc being wrought in Spain by the civil strife, was particularly interesting...

Great credit is due to Mr. Alguire for the really fine theatre, which he has given the town. Well constructed in every detail, the interior of the building is decorated in a light blue color, while decorative lights along the walls greatly enhance the lovely interior. The usherettes, Audrey Ryder and Gudrun Erickson, daintily attired in picturesque costumes of blue, trimmed with red, skillfully directed the patrons to the covered seats, which add greatly to the comfort of the patrons; as also does the sloping floor.

The sound equipment carried a very clear and true tone, while the picture itself was particularly clear, chiefly owing to the beaded sound screen with which the theatre is equipped. Construction of the entire building was under supervision of W.G. Chantler, pioneer builder and contractor of Whitehorse, who deserves credit for the excellent workmanship and structural design of the building.

I remember going with my Dad to this film. He laughed so loud at the comics in this and every show he saw later that the whole audience would be laughing with him.

Sports

One of the pleasures of my teenage years was playing basketball on the high school team. Softball was "out" for me, until Laurie Todd, our teacher, ordered a wire cage to protect my glasses. It helped me overcome the fear of a fastball hurtling towards my face. With basketball, however, I never had to use the thing, and the games were exciting with very intense competition.

Harold Macdonald, (who later married my late husband's sister) coached the girls' team. We called ourselves The Spitfires.

Once a year, in the fall, the Whitehorse school teams went over on the train to play against our neighboring town of Skagway, Alaska, 110 miles away by rail. We eagerly looked forward to this event all year long. The high school team would be billeted out to stay with the families of kids close to our own ages. After the games they had a party and dance in the school gym. The first "real" dance I ever went to was in Skagway, where a boy called J. D. True, acting as an unofficial host for his school, invited me to go with him. Neither one of us had learned to dance much—but it was a memorable occasion for me just the same.

I met a young soldier at the dance and ended up talking to him most of the evening. A lot of soldiers were being trained in the Chilkoot barracks square there at the time, before going overseas to active duty. This fellow was a long way from his home in Oklahoma and very lonely. He wanted someone to correspond with when he was away, he said, so we promised to exchange letters. I never saw the soldier again, but we did exchange a few letters and sent each other a snapshot, before he left Skagway. My mother thought I was much too young to be writing to a man.

Much too soon it was time for J. D. to take me home. He was a real brick about being so neglected at the party (probably relieved he didn't have to dance.) We joked and laughed on the way home, and it felt like a real date after all.

J. D. True later became an engineer on the White Pass Railway, a position he kept for forty years. In 1994 he published a book called *It Happened on the White Pass: The Life and Times of a Narrow-Gage Railway Engineer*. That was the same year he was appointed General Road-foreman of Steam by Paul Taylor, the Senior Vice President of White Pass.

The family I stayed with in Skagway had a bathroom with a flush toilet. It was the kind that had a water tank mounted on the wall with a pull chain on it. I eyed that chain with much trepidation, before finally getting the nerve to pull it. The water came pouring down with a loud rushing noise and just about scared me out of my wits. I remember running out into the hall, pulling up my pants as I ran.

My Brush with the Law

Back home again, we waited impatiently for Skagway's turn to come and play in Whitehorse. We tried to return their hospitality as best we could, with a smorgasbord in the Community Hall, followed by a school dance. All the kids thought the dance ended too soon, so a group of us decided to go for a dip in the swimming hole. As it was June, and daylight for almost twenty-four hours, we still weren't ready to call it quits, so off we traipsed up the bridle path and on to Ice Lake. There was Audrey, Gladys and I, a couple of other girls, and several boys from Skagway.

By the time we reached there, it was really getting late, and I was beginning to think of the consequences we would face when we got home. There were several cabins built around the lake by that time, and one of them belonged to the parents of one of the

Cabin that Dad built (Ice Lake, Yukon).

46

kids in our gang. Someone suggested we go in her cabin to see if there was any food available.

Gladys and I didn't like the idea, so we split up into two groups; the others got into the cabin somehow. I suddenly thought of all those good cookies Mom always kept at our cabin, just a short walk down the path. Hunger finally won over, and two of the Skagway boys tagged along to see whether or not we could get in.

The screen door was locked, of course, but we figured by pulling a few tacks out we could reach through the screen and open the other door, which we did. Those cookies tasted wonderful and gave us enough strength for the long trek back. Every step closer to home we got, the more frightened we became. It was three o'clock in the morning, and the novelty of "hanging out" with the Skagway boys had long since worn off. Besides, we reasoned, if we hadn't met up with them we wouldn't be in this perilous situation right now. When we reached town we quickly parted company.

Alone now, Gladys and I felt even more vulnerable. We decided we would face the music tomorrow. Tonight we would just spend what was left of the night in the vacant house that Gladys' family would be moving into in a day or two. Just before we reached the house a voice yelled, "Hey, wait up, your two!" Audrey and her friends had caught up with us. But Gladys and I had enough excitement for one night and only wanted to go and get some sleep.

"We have to make a pact," Audrey said, "I want you to promise, cross your heart and hope to die, that you'll never say a word to anyone, about where we were tonight, and I'll promise the same. Anyone who breaks this pact will be damned forever!"

Her voice was demanding and ominous (it was an act), and I felt a chill run up and down my spine. We all shook hands on it and went our separate ways. Gladys and I found some bed covers her mother had already moved over to the house and were asleep before our heads hit the pillow.

The next few days were traumatic to say the least. I was torn two ways, wanting to tell Mom and Dad about it. After all, I reasoned, the only thing we did wrong was eating up all those cookies, and the boys had made a sloppy job of fixing that screen

47

door; still, we had made a commitment to the others not to tell. To break that promise would be really tacky. So, I went around with a heavy heart and a lump in my throat.

Next day, horror of horrors, we got word that the people who owned the other cabin had notified the police, who, in turn, had talked to my parents. They immediately took a walk up to our cabin, saw the screen door and confirmed that, yes, our cabin had been broken into, too.

"The police will find them," they said. Now it was sheer terror Gladys and I felt, especially when, a couple of days later, the police questioned *us*. They asked things like, "What is your favorite chocolate bar?" and then produced an empty Coffee Crisp wrapper. How did they know we always bought those? I thought. We knew the jig was up, when they told us that Audrey had admitted to everything. So much for commitments, I thought; now we're criminals...

When I came home that day, there was a rebuke in the air you could cut with a knife. To this day I can see the hurt on my parent's faces. And I still feel the remorse of letting them down. We were all grounded after that for some time.

Dating Years

One of the best things about being a teenager, I think, is how hilarious life can be sometimes. We would laugh until our stomachs hurt and giggle uncontrollably at the least provocation. All down through the years I've noticed the same trait in younger teens everywhere. May it last forever, annoying as it may be at times for some adults. Life gets too serious soon enough.

Gladys and I decided it was her and me against the world, and we were best friends, sharing secrets and discussing very important topics, such as which boys were the best looking and what clothes we were going to save our money for (top priority in our lives just then). We could earn the odd dollar babysitting and splitting wood for my dad. Then we would get out the Eaton's mail-order catalogue and spend hours daydreaming.

"Hurry up, I can see the smoke now!" Gladys was balanced precariously on the top railing of the fence, eyes squinting against the sun as she gazed toward the Yukon River, just barely visible from her vantage point. She had been waiting for a glimpse of the SS *Casca*, which was due to arrive at the White Pass dock in about ten minutes.

"Well," I answered, "if you'd get off your butt and give me a hand here I'd be finished sooner." Splitting the wood in our backyard for the morning's kindling was my job after school, a way to earn spending money. Just as I raised the axe above my head one more time, three blasts from the steam whistle of the paddlewheeler sounded loud and clear, piercing the hot summer air. A little shiver of excitement ran up my spine and the woodpile was forgotten as I pulled Gladys off the fence.

"I'll finish it later. Come on!" We ran the three blocks to the river, where the boat was just pulling up to the wharf. The year was 1941, and we were both fifteen years old, a fact that we kept to ourselves as much as possible. We were sure we could easily pass for sixteen. We jostled our way through the crowd on the dock in order to get a glimpse of the young deckhands on board.

"Look," Gladys said, "there's the same two who waved at us last time. I think they're looking at us." The thought was enough to keep us daydreaming for the rest of the day. The boys at school were so immature, we decided, and we wouldn't date them if they were the last ones on earth. We ignored the fact that they had not asked us to anyway.

Actually, we could pass for a year or two older, and some of the young deckhands on the paddlewheelers would bend over backwards to get our attention, while we would feign great indifference. Eventually we got acquainted with two fellows on the *Casca* and two more on the *Klondike*. The movie theatre in town was our major source of entertainment. As long as we were home by nine-thirty our folks were reluctantly tolerant.

Because all the steamboats on the river arrived and left on different days, Gladys and I were going to quite a few movies, which we really enjoyed. Luckily, the "moccasin telegraph" never caught up with us, so the fellows all thought they were the only ones taking us out on dates. After a month or two of this, though, we settled for the two we liked best and never bothered with the others.

We never tired of watching the boats come and go, and many of the Whitehorse folks seemed to feel the same way, as there was always quite a gathering of people standing on the White Pass dock in the summertime. It was an end to cabin fever until next winter rolled around. There was something about the thrust of that paddlewheel, as we watched the ship back away from the wharf. The pilot up there in the pilot house, one hand on the big steering wheel and the other reaching up to blow the whistle, held us spellbound. The smokestacks billowed out a white plume of steam and smoke that trailed along behind the vessel as it slowly pulled out of town on its way to Dawson City. The rivers were our only highways in those days, and the White Pass train that ran from Skagway to Whitehorse was our only link to the outside world.

All too soon the season ended, and it was time for the crews to leave for the "Outside" again. The year was now 1942, and that fall, our girls' basketball team rode the same train that the boat crews were taking, going back to their homes in B.C. We said goodbye to our friends when we reached Skagway and rushed to the school to practice for the upcoming games.

On our trip back to Whitehorse I met a tall, handsome man. He started a conversation, and all too soon the train was pulling into the station, where I said a reluctant goodbye, never dreaming that this was the man with whom I would spend many years of my life.

3

Fast Forward

I had met Gordon when I was 15 years of age. I was dreading the day he would insist on knowing how old I was. He'd asked me, but I'd always managed to avoid answering, giving a nonsensical answer, and then changing the subject. I had my friends sworn to secrecy, but it couldn't last forever. The fact that I was interested, I hoped, would also remain a secret. If he found out how young I was — well, I just didn't know how he'd feel. So I agonized day and night, putting off the inevitable day when he would demand that I tell him.

And then suddenly it was over. A week went by and I never heard a word, or saw a sign of him. I had never been so miserable in my life. I dragged myself to school, and tried to concentrate on my lessons. It was impossible. Although I read the words with my eyes, my brain would just not process them at all. Luckily it wasn't exam time, because my marks would have been very bad.

One day on my way to school, I turned the corner by the old log church, and there he was, coming toward me. Composing my face, I quickly made up my mind not to stop at all. I'd just smile coolly, I thought, give him a bright "Hi," and keep right on going. I would have rather died than let him think it *mattered* that he hadn't tried to contact me for seven days. He had probably found out from someone that I was really only fifteen. But he stopped and said, "Well, imagine meeting you here!"

My feet refused to go on, but I said with marvelous restraint, "Oh, this is the route I always take to school."

"I'll sure be glad to get off this damn shift, so things can get

51

back to normal. I've missed you," he continued. "Let's get together on Sunday. I have two days off, then I'm back on days again."

I didn't walk; I floated on air the rest of the way to school. And again it was impossible to concentrate, but at least the reason this time was joy, and not misery as before.

By some quirk of fate, I just happened to run into Gordon for the next three days in exactly the same place and at the same time. Every morning I'd be a little later for school, and every afternoon before I could go home I'd cheerfully write on the board a hundred times, "*I must not be late for school*" over and over, happily humming to myself and dreaming of the weekend.

A year later we were married in the old log church.

The next fifty-eight years of my life were spent married to Gordon Yardley, and are covered by my book, published in 1993, entitled *Crazy Cooks and Gold Miners*. Here, then, is a brief outline of some of the other highlights that occurred in my life, both prior to and after that time period.

Before I met Gordon, he had worked on the paddle wheeler, SS *Tutshi*, which had a tourist run from Carcross, down Tagish Lake, to Ben-My-Chree. Every winter, he returned to his home in Langley, B.C. In 1941, he found steady work as a mechanic for Pan American Airlines in Whitehorse.

And, of course, in 1942 along came the huge influx of American soldiers to work on the Alcan Highway, as it was called then, from Whitehorse to Alaska. Needless to say, the town underwent an abrupt cultural shock overnight.

Gordon and I were married that year in July. The next spring we moved to Carcross, so he could take on an army contract to supply telephone poles from Skagway, Alaska, to Whitehorse.

In 1945, we bought "10 Mile Ranch," on Tagish Lake. We raised beef cattle; fished commercially for the *Tutshi*; put up hay and kept a number of riding horses. And last, but not least, we raised three children, Norma, Kirk, and Ted. I taught Norma by correspondence for the first two years, then we moved back to Carcross where we had built a home. I was Postmistress there for five years.

In 1960 we left Carcross, and bought a tourist lodge, 200

miles by road, southwest on the Haines Highway at Dezadeash Lake. We carried on that operation for eight years. Our next venture was trapping for lynx and wolverine for two winters with our snow machines. In 1975 we built a permanent home in Whitehorse, close to our daughter Norma and her husband Cal Waddington.

Gordon and our son Kirk formed a construction company, involving trucks and earth-moving equipment. I was fortunate enough to become enrolled in two art courses, one in sketching and one in pottery, from the well-known artist Ted Harrison. By 1977, the building boom had subsided, and Gordon, Kirk, and Ted tried a new venture — gold mining in Atlin, B.C. This was to be our life for the next fifteen years, part of that time spent in the Mt. Freegold area near Carmacks and, in 1986, in the goldfields near Dawson City, Yukon.

My husband suffered a severe stroke in 1981, and Kirk and Ted carried on at the mine. In 1987 we sold our home in Whitehorse, and bought a house in Saltair, Vancouver Island. Then we sold the mine and retired. In 1993 bought a condo in Nanaimo.

My husband Gordon Yardley passed away on September 20, 2000. Time does heal the pain, thank goodness, and today I sit here writing my memoirs, having embarked on another wonderful phase of my life.

In December 2002, I married for the second time to a close friend who had lost his partner a year previously. Already our experiences together would almost fill another book, and we are thankful that life has been kind in allowing us this second chance at happiness.

The following chapter is a collection of short Yukon stories my late husband liked to tell. Most took place in the 1940s.

4
Yukon Vignettes

I've stood in some mighty-mouthed hollow
That's plumb-full of hush to the brim;
I've watched the big, husky sun wallow
In crimson and gold, and grow dim.

— ROBERT SERVICE

Fred Lawson

Mr. and Mrs. Fred Lawson lived on Tagish Lake, at Hail City, just across the lake from Golden Gate. The first time I saw Fred, he was standing on his wharf watching as our boat pulled up alongside. He made an imposing picture—all 6'4" of him silhouetted against the sky, as we sat there looking up at him. He put me in mind of a Viking, with his broad-brimmed fisherman's hat, the wind whipping his shoulder-length white hair and his face deeply tanned and lined from the sun.

He recognized Gordon and greeted us warmly, at the same time reaching for the rope and securing it to a piling. The Lawsons had lived at this picturesque location for forty-eight years.

The SS *Tutshi* used to stop here twice a year; the first and last trip of the summer season. It brought them mail and supplies, mostly dry food such as flour, sugar, baking powder, etc. They raised their own garden vegetables, and the lake and forest supplied them with fish and meat. Fred took us inside to meet his wife, Agnes (he called her Willie), an energetic little woman who bustled around a spotless kitchen while making us tea. We had a pleasant afternoon, listening to their stories and walking around the well-kept garden. I had never seen such large, luscious straw-berries.

Fred trapped in the winter and did a little mining in the summer months. During the course of the conversation, the remark, "Was that before or after Reggie brought in the cow, Fred?" or, "I believe that happened the same year Reggie brought in the cow," came up quite frequently. We began to realize that they were referring to a very important event in their lives. Finally we asked them about it.

The residents along the lake had never kept any farm animals, due to the expense of bringing in feed for them. Most kept mink or foxes that, of course, were fed with fish from the lake. One memorable winter in the 1930s, Reggie Brooks had brought in a cow from the Outside. He had shipped it up from Vancouver to Skagway, then over the railway to Carcross. From there it was loaded onto a "stoneboat" and pulled over the lake by dogteam. (A stoneboat is a flat-bottomed sled with runners and a wooden deck.). It had been quite an undertaking, and ever since then folks had used the incident as a kind of milestone by which to gauge a time span.

"How long has it been since you took a trip Outside, Fred ?" I asked.

"Oh, not too long," he replied. "I went to Skagway (sixty-seven miles away) to get my teeth fixed...let's see... couldn't have been more than twelve years ago."

A year or so after our visit, the Lawsons moved to Atlin. They were getting on in years, and the town people were concerned about them living so far from help should it be needed, especially with no telephone facilities. They made the move reluctantly; this had been home to them for so long. It also meant an end to their means of livelihood. Fred decided they would have to apply for the old age pension. When they went to see about it, though, they discovered that Agnes wasn't eligible; she was born in the United States and had never obtained her Canadian citizenship. In order for them both to receive the pension they would have to get married.

This came as a real surprise to the Atlinites; they had always surmised that the Lawsons had enjoyed that holy state for forty-nine years or so. Soon all the legalities were taken care of and they settled down in Atlin. Willie happily adjusted to the social life in town. For the first time in years she could truly indulge in her favorite pastime—talking. She even joined a group of ladies for afternoon bridge twice a week.

Fred found it a bit harder, and time dragged a lot, especially when Willie was out "with the girls." One day he came in the house at five o'clock for his dinner, as he had done for so many years, but Willie was not home yet. When she arrived half an hour later, he let it be known that he was not pleased with this behavior. Willie promised sweetly that it wouldn't happen again, and he was mollified for a time. Only a week later, the same thing happened. When his wife came in the door he was ready for her.

"Look here, woman," he exclaimed, "I've always had my dinner on time, and I'm not about to wait around for it now that you're my wife. I'll expect it on time from now on, and that's an order!"

Little Willie drew herself up to her full height, turned on her heel and stalked out of the house. She booked herself into the hotel and refused to go back home. After much persuasion by the town folk the old couple patched things up again. It was their first argument in almost fifty years.

Ernie Butterfield

Ernie Butterfield lived at 10 Mile Ranch on Tagish Lake. He raised mink for a living, and the lake supplied him with all the white fish and trout he needed to feed them. Once in a while though, he had to go into the little town of Carcross, fourteen miles west, to shop for various other supplies and food.

He told Gordon about one exceptionally cold winter day when he had to make one of these trips by dogteam. He was glad he had worn his long buffalo robe coat, especially when a blizzard came up while crossing the section of the lake known as Windy Arm. The very first thing he did when he got into town that morning was tie up his dogs and then dive into the lobby of the Caribou Hotel to warm up.

Just as he walked up to the warm heater, a traveler who had overnighted at the hotel came downstairs shivering from the cold. The old hotel didn't have much in the way of heat upstairs; over the years the sawdust insulation had all sunk down to the lower level. Still half asleep, the traveler also headed for the wood heater and stretched his arms out to the crackling wood burner. Suddenly, he became aware of big Ernie, hugging the stove on the other side, buffalo robe all matted with snow and icicles hanging from his eyebrows and nose. The little man looked up, shocked and amazed. He said, "My God! What room did you have here last night?"

Just then the train whistled, and the man wheeled around to run upstairs, where he had left his teeth overnight in the jug of cold water on the nightstand in his room. To his dismay, he discovered that the water had frozen solid overnight, and he could not recover his false teeth without thawing it. Trouble was there was no time for this, because the train was leaving right away. So he picked up jug and all and tore downstairs; out the front door of the hotel, heading for the train station.

Bobby Robson, the proprietor, saw this happening, and took off out the door in hot pursuit.

"Stop...stop!" he shouted, "Thief! My jug!" The little man just kept running, but turned his head and yelled, "I'm sorry, Sir, my teeth are in it.... I'll return it to you soon as I get home." Big Ernie said that Bobbie was so upset, he went to the bar and downed a double whiskey.

The Harlan Brothers

The Harlan brothers, Jack and Norm, were trappers living at Moose Arm on Tagish Lake. Once a year they would sell a bunch of furs, pool their resources and then go to Carcross for a party. Theirs was no ordinary party. This was sometimes a $14,000-binge! People for miles around would wait eagerly for this one (that is, of course, the ones who liked to celebrate in this fashion—there were others who just hoped they wouldn't come back).

The first thing they did was to rent three rooms in the Caribou Hotel, one for each of them and one in the middle for the "beer room." Then they ordered in a barrel of beer and a case of overproof rum and held open house for anyone in town who wanted to come. In those days, beer used to come by the barrel, with about seventy-two quart bottles in each one. When a barrel was empty, they just ordered another. The celebration went on, with much noise and rowdiness, until all their money was gone, and they and their friends went home to nurse huge hangovers for a day or two and trap more furs.

One day, before we were married, Gordon went down the lake to see old Ernie Butterfield. When it was time to leave, he hiked to Carcross, with the intention of taking the train back to Whitehorse. He just missed it by fifteen minutes. He was in the Caribou Hotel, contemplating his next move, when Norm Harlan came over. Norm was a good-looking, well-built man in his fifties, permanently tanned from months of sun and wind, trapping and dog-mushing on the lake in the winter.

"I'm looking for a ride to Whitehorse," Norm said. "Know of anyone going in?" He told Gordon that a couple of days ago, in Whitehorse (where he was now living), he had gone to the train station to see a pal of his off to Vancouver. The train was leaving in twenty minutes, so they just had time enough for a couple of farewell drinks. Norm decided to take his bottle and join his friend on the train, where it was comfortable, till it was time to get off.

The time passed so quickly that before he realized what was happening, they were already several miles out of town. He figured he would have to go on to Carcross and come back the next day. The next day he sat around the bar, waiting for the train. Somehow, he missed it. Now it was going to be several days before another one came along, and here he was, like Gordon, without a ride back to Whitehorse.

Jack MacMurphy was the foreman of the Carcross section crew at that time. He was also authorized to take passengers over the railway to Whitehorse, if the demand came up, on the "Casey," a little open, flatbed on wheels that ran on the track to ensure it was clear of any obstructions. The Casey had a one-cylinder motor, cooled with an open water jacket. Norm decided the only thing left to do was hire Jack to take him to Whitehorse; the fare was $35. Gordon offered to go with him and split the cost.

From Carcross to Lorne it is uphill all the way, and the motor was pretty hot before they got that far. Jack mentioned they would probably have to stop and let it cool off. Once on top, there was a creek where they could drain the water jacket and fill it again with cold water. While they waited for the motor to cool,

Norm pulled out a bottle of beer from the ample supply he had brought with him and took a long drink.

"Why couldn't we drain the motor here and fill her with beer?" he asked.

"Never tried it before, but guess it could be done. Let's give it a try," Jack said. They continued on to the top of the grade. After awhile, the beer started to get hot and flow over the top of the open water jacket; dropping big globs of sudsy foam on the track behind them. Norm sat there watching the beer flow out, a contented look on his face. After awhile he reached into the foam with two grimy fingers, took a lick and smacked his lips.

"Sa-a-ay, that's ALL RIGHT," he said.

The Bush Pilots

Commercial flying out of Whitehorse began in 1928. Some outstanding pilots came north and contributed to the early history of aviation in the Yukon. Clyde Wann started the Yukon Airways and Exploration Co., and Lieutenant A. D. Cruikshank piloted their first plane, *Queen of the Yukon*, up to Whitehorse on October 25, 1927. It was a Ryan B-1 Monoplane, a sistership to the *Spirit of St. Louis*, the aircraft that Charles Lindberg used (also in 1927) on the nonstop flight across the Atlantic.

In May of 1928, the *Queen* crash-landed on a return flight from Mayo, Keno and Dawson, due to extremely strong winds. Fortunately, the pilot and two passengers were not hurt. The plane was replaced by the *Northern Light*, an open-cockpit biplane. Next came the *Queen of the Yukon II*, which crashed on the Stewart River on November 2, 1929, this time killing the pilot.

Many bush pilots were flying up north in the 1930s and 1940s. The ones that I remember most were Jess Rice, Frank Barr, Von Woods, Vern Brookwalter, Everett Wasson and Les Cook—outstanding flyers, all of them. There were several incidences of pilots getting lost in the bush during bad storms. In those days the search was given up after five or six days (relatively short by today's standards), but the men often came trudging back home two or three weeks later, their clothes in rags, hungry as bears, but still alive. Men of true grit, they flew their single-motored airplanes sometimes in -40°F with only a part-cowling and in some cases none at all—just the cylinders sticking out in the wind, the oil as stiff as tar. Pilot and plane took quite a beating in conditions such as this.

Places like Teslin and Ross River were pretty isolated before the Alaska Highway was built, especially before the bush pilots began servicing them. Where now it takes two hours driving to Teslin from Whitehorse, it used to take several days to go by dogteam, and longer yet to hike it on snowshoes. No wonder a sack of flour that sold for $5 in Whitehorse would be $30 at the Teslin Trading Post.

In the winter months the pilots flew trappers and supplies back and forth, landing on the rivers or lakes with skis. In summer, the passengers were mostly prospectors and miners. Then pontoons would take the place of skis on the aircraft. The problems the pilots encountered were endless when fighting the cold, especially keeping the motors heated between flights and coping with poor visibility. Many times when it was exceptionally bad, they would have to fly really low and just hedge-hop above the trees until the airfield came into view.

Even though a few pilots did get lost, there were those who just seemed to have the homing instinct. The most outstanding of these being Les Cook, who started off flying for George Simmons, owner and operator of Northern Airways, out of Carcross. Les had received his training in the Canadian Air Force, but was discharged when it was discovered that he was color-blind, even though it didn't handicap him in the least. So he decided to come north and be a bush flyer.

On the first day he went to work for George, he flew from Carcross to Teslin, from Teslin to Ross River, on to Sheldon Lake and back to Carcross with absolutely no trouble at all. That's a lot of mountainous country for a stranger to tackle on his first flight in the area, but Les had that uncanny instinct that never seemed to fail him.

In 1941 Les moved to Whitehorse and went flying for the U.S. Air Force. He had always been a daredevil flyer, but once he confided to a friend that the only thing he feared was fire. He was given a Norseman to fly, and his luck finally ran out when he came to a tragic end in a fiery crash on a street in Whitehorse.

There were many unsung heroes in those early years before

the Alaska Highway—men of great stamina and resourcefulness, who traveled by land and air, hauling freight and supplies around the country. My late husband, Gordon, was always fascinated by the tales some of these rugged pioneers could tell, some of which I will try to do justice to in the following paragraphs.

Before the Highway

By 1928 transportation on the old Dawson Trail between Whitehorse and Dawson City had been upgraded from horses to Caterpillars. It was nearly 400 miles to Dawson, at that time the capital of the Yukon. At the turn of the century it had been one of the larger cities this side of Winnipeg, due of course to the Klondike Gold Rush.

A tremendous number of people went south for the winter in those days, catching the last trip of the season on the paddle-wheelers from Dawson to Whitehorse, then over the railway to Skagway, where they boarded a steamship to Vancouver or Seattle. Many of them stayed out only a couple of months before they wanted to come back to the Yukon. Once they arrived again in Whitehorse they had to travel in open sleighs, sometimes in -40°F, all the way to Dawson. The Cat drivers would try to keep them warm between roadhouses by piling buffalo skin robes over and around them.

My school chum, Gladys, and I loved to catch a ride on one of these "Cat Trains" in the mid-1930s. If the weather was mild, Louis Mois the driver, would let us stay on and ride a couple of miles out of town on the sleigh. We would snuggle under the robes with the other passengers and pretend we were going all the way to Dawson, that romantic town we had heard so many stories about. Louis would stop and shoo us off while we were still within safe walking distance from town.

Later in the season, when the snow became packed hard, trucks could sometimes be used to replace Cats on the Dawson Trail and on access roads to the scattered wood camps as well.

Aimes (Happy) LePage, a local contractor, took on a job with the White Pass to supply part of the thousands of cords of wood that would be used to operate the steamboats that ran on the Yukon River in the summer months, namely the SS *Klondike*, *Casca*, *Whitehorse* and *Aksala*.

The wood had to be cut as close to the river as possible, and Happy hired a crew of men to help him. They skid the logs out of the bush and piled it in stacks on the river bank, where much later boat crews would load it onboard the steamboats, using two-wheeled carts called "trucks," pushing them by hand over ramps made from gangplanks. The firemen on the boats fired up the furnaces that created the steam that powered the engines.

Happy started off using a horse to skid the logs out of the bush. In later years, he progressed to single-wheel trucks, rigged out with flat decks for loading purposes. As an additional source of income he supplied firewood to the people in Whitehorse. One day Happy, accompanied by Louis Mois, and with a truckload of firewood, started back to town. They came as far as the Takhini River, which was frozen over, and attempted to cross it on the ice.

The river here is maybe 200 to 300 yards across. In the wintertime, an overflow of water will often flood the ice and then freeze. This is called glaciering, and this time it had caused a two- or three-inch crust to form on the surface. Under this crust was water, which lay on the ice and made it very porous.

Trucks were apt to break through while trying to cross, as these two drivers found out this particular afternoon. They dropped through the shell ice and into a water hole two and a half feet deep. In attempting to get out, they broke their universal joint, which left them powerless. They were still about thirty miles out of town, and the weather had turned too cold to leave the truck for any length of time. If it froze up there in the water they would have a major chore to get it out. The drivers were always wise enough to carry warm, dry clothes with them and spare parts for the motor. These men even had an extra universal along. The trouble was, they had no way to get the thing switched over, as the water and shell ice was just about up to the frame of the truck. It was a matter of fixing it right where it was or possibly face losing the truck. So they hatched the only scheme that they figured would work.

Most anybody in their right mind would have given up any hope of fixing that truck there in the middle of the river at -40°F but not these two men. They built a huge fire on the nearest shore. Happy LePage ducked under that freezing water and up under the truck. Once he got in between the frame, he could reach the universal, and he worked as long as he could without air, which was about two minutes. Then, he would get out and over to the fire, where he warmed up, while Louis Mois took his turn and did the same thing.

It must have taken them about an hour, but by taking turns like this beside the fire—their clothes steaming; rubbing their hands and stomping their feet to keep the circulation going—they actually managed to unbuckle that old universal and install the new one. Then they changed into dry clothes and drove into Whitehorse.

Don't Touch Those Brakes!

Truckers on the Alaska Highway back in the forties and fifties encountered some rather scary experiences at times, brought on by hazardous road conditions and very sparse traffic in the winter months. One time on his way to Dawson Creek, Gordon came upon a poor fellow in a big semitruck, whose trailer had jack-knifed when it spun out on a steep grade. The outfit slid around on the ice and was now facing uphill. The driver thought he had a broken axle, so there he sat all night long; tensely holding the brakes with his foot and waiting for someone to come along.

Gordon stopped to help the trucker, who by then was white faced and staring straight ahead, as though by turning his head he might start sliding back down the hill. By trying out all the gears, it turned out that the auxiliary transmission had slipped out of gear when the truck hit the bank. There was nothing wrong with the axle. Gordon hooked onto the trailer, lined it up on the road, and the embarrassed trucker was on his way again.

Fred Boss sitting on top of a freight truck that had broken through the ice, Takhini Crossing.
PHOTO: Yukon Archives, Whitehorse, print #1910.

You Work or Else

The SS *Tutshi* carried tourists back and forth to the end of Tagish Lake from Carcross, Yukon, to a beautiful little oasis called Ben-My-Chree (a Manx expression for "girl of my dreams") at the end of the lake. On one of its runs, the boat had to layover for a day at Taku Arm to clean out the boilers. First, though, the crew had to take the freight that was onboard over the two and a half miles of railway, where it was barged across Atlin Lake by the *Norgold*, the boat used by the White Pass Co. for that purpose. Gordon helped with the freight this day and went along for the ride to Atlin, B.C., where he was free to roam around and look the town over. He wandered down to the wharf, where an old-timer was preparing to go out with his sixteen-foot boat to run his fish nets.

"Hi, young feller, would you like to come along and see how it's done?" he asked.

"I think I'll take you up on that," Gordon replied.

The old fisherman bent down to start up his motor. He was using an old-style Evinrude, with a square gas tank and a knob starter, the forerunner of the starting rope that is still in use today. This day luck was against him. He tried and tried to start the motor, but it would only fire half a dozen times and then stall. He stopped, pushed his old wide-brimmed hat up on his perspiring brow and flexed his hands, which were turning red with the right one showing the promise of a blister.

"Can't figure out why she won't start," he said, "she always started before."

Back he went for another try. Finally he gave up. He looked at his hands again in frustration, then abruptly made up his mind. "To hell with you!" he yelled. "If you won't work, you won't ride!" With that he unbuckled the motor, pulled it off and chucked it into the deep blue water. Then, satisfied, he calmly picked up his oars and rowed out to his nets.

Pioneers

Herb Auld had been a close friend of ours for many years. His home was in 100 Mile House, B.C., where he had lived since he was a young man. He started the first business in what was then just a small village. Herb was a big, jovial man with a ready laugh and a genuine liking for people. We have traveled together by car a few times, through the States and down into Mexico, and the number of friends and acquaintances he knew wherever we stopped was truly amazing. He remembered everything about the folks he had met over the years, including the names of their children. Needless to say, he was well liked and respected by them all.

Herb was also a shrewd businessman. He built the 100-Mile Garage and Service Station and, with his son Tommy, turned it into a thriving business. For many years they had the Toyota dealership and parts department. Herb knew everyone in town (before it expanded into the city it is now) and was aware of their individual interests and problems. He was known for extending considerable credit in those days.

Behind the garage, there was a lot in which he kept old cars and pickups, mostly trade-ins waiting to be repaired or sold for parts. On Saturday nights after a dance or drinking binge, some of the town's hardiest revelers would end up "sleeping it off" in one of these vehicles.

A couple of the employees, having been hired only recently, were quite irritated the first time they discovered these bodies snoring away in the back lot and were in the process of booting them out of there when Herb came along.

"What's going on here, anyway?" he asked them. "Who told you to hassle these fellows? Leave them alone, they're not hurting anyone!"

Gordon and I were visiting Herb one time, and just as we were approaching the garage, a couple of local characters were weaving past us, trying to hold each other up and having a heated argument at the same time.

"I need a drink or I gonna pass out right here," one of them was saying.

"No way, man, you come to Herbie's Hotel, right now!" his partner scolded.

Knowing nothing about the back lot, I looked at Gordon in amazement. "Does Herb have a hotel, too?"

"Sure," he said, "right behind the garage!"

Henry was one of the regular guests of Herbie's Hotel on Saturday nights. He used to leave the beer parlor at closing time and go home but always ended up getting in a fight with Mary, his wife, and beating her up, so she began locking him out when he was drinking, and he was forced to resort to Herbie's.

One day Henry came to a tragic end in an automobile accident. Herb never missed a funeral when one of the townspeople passed on. He, and a friend who was visiting, took time to go to this one. They gave us an account of it later.

The service was held in the Catholic church. There were many tearful friends there; in the front pew was Henry's wife with her new boyfriend. A short, stocky woman, she sat there reeking slightly of rye whiskey with a sullen expression on her round face. Both her moccasin-clad feet were planted firmly on the floor, and she was chewing gum with determination.

The minister began his eulogy with the usual condolences to friends and family, and then continued: "Henry was a hard working man, and..."

"Bull shit!" she retorted.

There was shocked silence. Then the minister said in a soothing tone, "Now, now, you don't mean that. You're upset; that is understandable. Henry had his weaknesses, but he was always kind to his family and..."

"Bull shit!" she said again, only louder this time.

Red-faced, the embarrassed clergyman quickly brought the service to a close and announced the last hymn.

How the North was Won

I think one of the most interesting people we came across in our life in the Yukon was Jimmy Kane. Jimmy started out in the village of Nesketaheen, which later became Dalton Post. At that time no white men had arrived in that part of the country, but the northern coastal Indians, the Tlingets, used to hike over a trail (later called the Dalton Trail) to trade with the Interior tribes.

When Jack Dalton and his partner showed up in the village for the first time the Natives thought they were sick Indians, as their skin was so pale; so they didn't want to get too close for fear they would catch a disease.

At that time the Indians already had a few old muzzle-loaders, guns that they had got from the coast Indians in trade for fur. Dalton's men had what Jimmie described as "little short gun, they tie him on their hip." They could pull out one of these and fire six shots. Jack Dalton at this time began to establish his famous trading post and a trail that eventually branched out to the West and came out near the Kluane district at the White River. Another branch ran north through Champagne and the Hutshi country, a district named by the Indians and meaning in their language, "end of the trail." The trail gradually was extended to the Yukon River, becoming one of the routes to the Klondike gold fields. It became known as the famous Dalton Trail.

The horses brought over this trail were the first ones seen by the Klukshu Indians. They kept their distance at first, as the closest comparison they had to this animal was, of course, the native moose, and they expected the same reaction from the horses, that they would run away if they tried to approach them.

Dalton had brought tea, coffee, sugar and flour among other things when they arrived. Jimmy and his people knew what tea was from trading with the Tlingets, but coffee was still unknown to them.

"Jack Dalton, he say coffee good for heart," Jimmy said. "Pretty soon you walk by tents in village—all you can smell that coffee cooking! He teach us make bannock from that flour, too, oh good, that bannock."

One day Gordon asked Jimmy about the old muzzle-loaders they used to have before Dalton's time. Apparently they were quite heavy, and to load one you had to stand it on the butt and drop black powder into the barrel, pound it down with a rod first, then push some wadding down and pack it in tight. Then some buckshot would have to be poured in and more wadding to hold it in place. The gun had a little pouch on the barrel to hold a small amount of black powder for igniting the load.

To shoot a moose with one of these guns, you had to get a bead on the animal first, then pull the trigger, which hit the flint, which ignited the powder in the pouch, which sizzled a while and finally went off with a boom! That old muzzle-loader was pretty heavy, and it wasn't easy to keep a bead on the moose while waiting for the powder to ignite. Especially when the mosquitoes were swarming all over a hunter's face!

Jimmy said, "You spot moose, he look right at you. You hold muzzle-loader and you wait, and wait...mosquitoes all over you face...you wait, drive you crazy, you know? By 'n by that moose he turn sideways. You shoot him quick and he go down. You throw that gun down and you reach up and quick mop those mosquitoes and blood off you face! Oh, that pretty bad..."

Gordon asked Jimmy, "Were your people upset by the white man coming into your country? Did you ever try to drive him away?"

Jimmy said, "No-o-o, well, first time we think sometime about that. Well, you know, we just have old muzzle-loaders. Jack Dalton, those men that time, they got little six-shooters on their hip—bang, bang, bang, bang, bang, bang."

Jimmy turned his hands up and shrugged his shoulders in resignation.

"What the hell we gonna do?" he said.

Mrs. Vioux's Rifle

During the war years in Whitehorse there was a period when everyone of German nationality was asked to turn in any firearms they had in their possession to the RCMP. When the owner of the White Pass Hotel, Mrs. Vioux, was told of this, she flat-out refused. Gordon's brother-in-law, Mac, who was a policeman there at the time, was commandeered to go and collect whatever guns she possessed.

All hell broke out when he arrived at the door to ask for her rifle. It would be "over her dead body" or not at all. Mac asked her why she was so adamant about parting with the gun.

"I need it to clean my chimney," she insisted in her broken English. Then, seeing the puzzlement on his face, she motioned Mac to follow her upstairs. She grabbed her rifle in one of the rooms, then led him up a couple of flights of narrow stairs to the attic and out onto the roof. Sweat broke out on Mac's face as she loaded a shell into the barrel of the gun, and it was with some relief he watched her take a bead on the smokestack. Bang! Bang! The holes she made joined a few others in the top of the chimney and "swoosh!" an accumulation of soot let go and slid down inside the pipe. Triumphantly, Mrs. Vioux turned to him and asked, "You see what I mean?" With a sigh of resignation, Mac threw up his hands and departed.

Prospecting Then and Now

The first prospectors to go up on the White Channel in Dawson caused everyone down below to laugh hilariously at the "fools," but they started digging anyway. They discovered an old riverbed up there that turned out to be the second great discovery in the Klondike. There was a whole new bonanza to be staked, just a mile or two away from the original discovery.

The old prospectors had a nose for gold that was phenomenal. A lot of them had been in the bush all their lives and they had developed eyes that recognized all the signs of mining activity that went on years before them. They uncovered creeks all grown over with brush and trees, and they could read the ground without the benefit of modern geological technology or instruments. They had an unerring ability to sink a shaft down in the right place. We saw lots of them when we were mining. Sometimes we would move twenty or thirty feet of overburden, in what we thought was virgin ground, and there would be a shaft.

They did it all by hand, digging long tunnels with pick and shovel, building small fires to thaw out the permafrost and then winching what they hoped was pay dirt to the surface to run through their primitive sluice boxes. Most of the modern-day prospectors couldn't begin to keep up to those old-timers when it comes to perseverance and back-breaking work under nearly impossible conditions.

Robert Service really captured the essence and spirit of these men in this stanza of his poem, "The Spell of the Yukon."

I wanted the gold and I sought it
I scrabbled and mucked like a slave,
Was it famine or scurvy I fought it.
I hurled my youth into a grave.
I wanted the gold and I got it;
Came out with a fortune last fall;
But somehow life's not what I thought it,
And somehow the gold isn't all.

— ROBERT SERVICE

5

Travels to Far-Away Places

Our Trip to Mexico

On the first of February, 1990, we left Desert Hot Springs on our way to Los Mochis, Mexico. We stopped overnight at Blythe, Arizona, and continued the next day to Quartzite, where the annual jamboree (Gemboree, they call it) was in full swing. It was the largest gem show and flea market in North America at that time; over half a million RVs converge each year around the small town of Quartzite, population 1,000.

Rock hounds and semiprecious stone buyers from all over the world came to look, barter and, in general, have a rollicking good time. Square dancing goes on all day and in the evenings as well. The trailers, motor homes, tents and fifth wheels spread out in all directions, as far as the eye can see.

The Main Event and the Big Tent are like huge trade shows. There are hundreds of "tailgaters" as well-people selling from their pickup trucks. Rows and rows of booths are setup to sell merchandise from all over the world. Musicians are everywhere, adding to the festive atmosphere.

When the show is all over (I think it lasts ten days) the traffic starts moving out, and the desert town returns to its peace and solitude until next year.

To see it all in detail, we would have had to stay for at least three days, but we were anxious to get to Mexico, so a few hours later we headed south again. Just past Yuma, we stopped to pick

Inside the cathedral.

up car insurance at San Luis. It was almost twenty years since we were in Mexico for any length of time, so we inquired as to what would be needed at the border. We were told we would need documents in the form of a vehicle permit and a tourist visa. The fellow said we should insist that we get them, otherwise we may be stopped at another checkpoint 150 miles farther on and made to return to the border for documentation. I was glad we had asked, because, sure enough, at the border they tried to just wave us on through.

We stopped and parked, went back and said, "We need a truck permit and tourist visa."

"Oh, si, si," the officer said, and we were ushered into a little back room in a building that had a makeshift door that wouldn't quite shut, one broken chair and a wooden desk with nothing on it but an old typewriter. There was a man in a brown suit who couldn't speak English, so he brought in another young man, dressed in a uniform jacket and blue jeans, who sat down at the desk and rummaged through all the drawers. Finally he started typing with two manicured fingers, filling out the forms.

He then came out with us to the truck and put a "*Tourista*" sticker on our windshield. We had to go to another "*officio*" for

Inside the cathedral.

our visas. At last we were on our way. We had no problems at the next checkpoint, where the offices (and officers) looked considerably more official than the ones at San Luis. We were stopped at another checkpoint, an agricultural inspection station. There was a woman there wearing a hard hat. She was carrying a white can with a red cross on it and was canvassing. I'm not sure what the hard hat was for...

At the third stop there were soldiers (Mexican with U.S. insignias on their jackets). One of them was standing guard with a rifle. The one that tried to talk to us couldn't speak English. When he realized we couldn't understand Spanish he just waved us on with a grin. We wondered what that was all about, although it was almost right at the Sinaloa-Sonora border. (On our way back, just before Santa Ana, we came to another checkpoint with a couple of armed soldiers. One was having a great time laughing and shooting at cans. They had "Narcotics" printed on their jackets. They just waved us on, too, as we still couldn't speak Spanish. Just going through the formalities, I guess.)

The Mexican countryside had changed very little in the previous twenty years. The people on the outskirts of cities were still living in a primitive fashion, as were most small villages; but we couldn't help but wonder if these people were really conscious of that fact. They went about their daily chores, the adults laughing and chatting. We saw many children running, shouting and chasing chickens. The burros were still pulling two-wheeled wooden trailers, or sometimes carrying the loads on their backs, packed with sticks for firewood or bundles of straw. Wherever there was a river, we could still see the women scrubbing clothes on the rocks and carrying baskets full of laundry on their heads. This habit, carried over from biblical times, was so entrenched that occasionally we would see women, even in the cities and in modern dress, standing at rest or just visiting with their shopping bags or packages on their heads.

The big change since we were there last was in the cities and the roads. Highway 15 was an excellent, paved four-lane freeway. The larger cities like Guaymas, Hermesilla, Cuidad Obregon and Los Mochis were still a mixture of the old and new, but the modern areas had grown immensely. A lot of the stores were comparable to ours; there were big supermarkets and some modern malls, huge banks and world-class hotels. Pure drinking water was available almost everywhere. The restrooms at gas stations ranged from crude to acceptable. We were wise enough to carry our own toilet paper, as their supply apparently ran out rather frequently.

Bartering for prices was a thing of the past now except at the outdoor markets, which were still as colorful as ever with Mexican music, brightly colored blankets and garments, leather

Inside the cathedral.

Hand-carved wooden bench.

belts, purses, pottery and wares of all descriptions. The cities teemed with pedestrians who ran the gamut between peasants and fashionable business people in suits and high heels. A lot of the teenagers dressed just like the Americanos, and we saw young girls in form-fitting white jeans and black cowboy boots. Everywhere you looked were immense shoe stores, "Canada" being one company and "Para Gon" the competition. The same company may have a store on both sides of the street right across from each other.

The Hotel Santa Anita, where we stayed in Los Mochis, charged $56 U.S. per night; it was very nice, with a large clean dining room that specialized in seafood, among other things. They had excellent coffee and a dessert cart with tempting choices of cakes and custards. Prices were much the same as in our country. Rooms offered valet and laundry services, and color television, with both English and Spanish channels. The lobby and dining room floors were beautiful polished marble. They also had a bar featuring live entertainment and top-ranking singers and bands. Before retiring to our room, we made arrangements to take a five-hour train tour on the railroad the next morning, through a wild and rugged canyon to a point called Bahuichivo. After breakfast the next day we got our last-minute instructions. We were told that a bus would meet us at the railway station and take us to the Hotel Mission in a small village about ten miles away. We were a bit surprised to see that we were the only ones getting off the train at this point. All the other passengers were going on further up the line, some to Creel and some to Chihuana. The train pulled away, leaving us there with a handful of Mexican men. Two of them came up to us in an old pickup with worn tires and said, "Hotel Mission?"

"Yes," we said. "We're waiting for the bus."

"Si!" one of them said, "Here's bus!" pointing to the pickup. He ushered us into the front seat. We looked at each other apprehensively. However, there was nothing else in sight. So here we were, miles from nowhere, up on a mountain in a strange county, driving along a crooked dirt road, through wild terrain with scrub-trees, cactus and eroded hills with massive boulders.

Some of these boulders had doors set in the deep crevices, and we found out later that they were Indian dwellings, still in use. An occasional burro and adobe shack dotted the trail, at long intervals between. Our drivers couldn't speak English, but we hoped they knew where they were taking us! After what seemed like hours, the truck jolted to a stop, and the driver got out and signaled to the other fellow in the back that they had to change a tire. Thank heaven they had a spare, was my first thought. Then I began to think that maybe this was the place

Everyone owns a burro.

75

where they pull out a gun and take our money and jewels...but I need not have worried. They had it fixed in jig time, and soon we were on our way again.

Finally, we came to an old, old village, primitive and yet neat in a way. The dirt yards were all swept clean of debris. Everyone had a few chickens strutting in and out of the adobe huts; most also had a couple of dogs and some burros. There were children everywhere. Some villagers had saddle horses and cows out in the pasture. Most of the women wore colorful skirts and scarves, and the little girls had frilly dresses and white socks.

Half an hour later we finally arrived at the hotel. The proprietors immediately sat us down to a delicious meal of vegetable soup, fresh-made warm corn tortillas and red snapper done in a fresh tomato sauce.

The "real" bus arrived just then, from a tour of Urique Canyon and the waterfalls. It had a load of "piggy-backers" as they were called—RV people who had a string of their motorhomes on a siding, back down at the railroad station from which we had come. They had started out from El Paso, Texas (the other end of the railway), to Chihuana, then by bus to Bahuichiva, where we were now. They had taken a side-trip to see the canyon, and now they were being seated family style, at

Inside the cathedral.

76

the long, wooden table where we were enjoying our meal. Some of them had showers, before returning (by real bus) to the station again. They were headed for Los Mochis, and then on to La Pas, Baja, in a day or two.

It was a pleasant dining room, with carved antique chairs in ironwood, and handmade brightly glazed pottery jugs filled with cold water on the table.

The train ride itself had been an unforgettable experience. We climbed to 6,000 ft. through lush green valleys, deep gorges and rugged mountains. They let us stand outside the cars on the platform. Where else, but in Mexico, would you be allowed to hang way over the edge and take pictures? Along the way we saw many different types of cacti and flowering trees we had never seen before. Some were called "cottonball" trees; no leaves this time of the year, but with puffs of cotton all over them. Others had lovely pink blossoms, some with golden yellow ones.

We crossed some very high bridges and went through many tunnels. The railway was completed in 1961 and had taken 100 years to build. It is a masterpiece of construction, an amazing accomplishment that opened up the Urique and Copper Canyons. Gordon spent most of the time standing outside, just taking it all in—a trip of a lifetime. I would like to go all the way to El Paso sometime. Apparently, some of the canyons are deeper than the Grand Canyon in Arizona. There are eighty-seven tunnels and thirty-nine bridges on the line.

The hotel Mision is built just about twenty feet from a massive, old Catholic mission founded by a Jesuit priest more than 300 years ago. It is very imposing, well preserved and still in use. The baptismal font is carved with pedestal and basin out of one piece of marble. It is also still in use in a little side room. The original gorgeous stained glass windows on either side of the altar are still like new, and the sculptures of Jesus, Mary and disciples are in excellent condition. It is kept open every day and we were allowed to go in and take pictures.

The hotel itself and the rooms were in white stucco with heavy brown wooden beams. There were carved oak furniture and doors with black wrought-iron decoration. Ours had a wrought-iron kerosene lamp stand, as well as an electric lamp, and a little wood heater with a skinny pipe reaching to the high

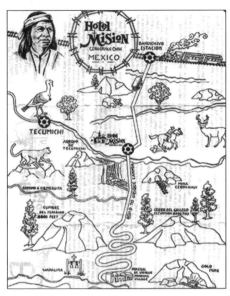

LEFT: *Hotel Mission, Los Mochis, Mexico.*

BELOW: *Third time today.*

78

Skinny little stovepipe.

ceiling. Alongside was a wooden box with split firewood. We were glad of it when darkness came; at that altitude it dropped to almost freezing at night. They only use the electricity for four hours in the evening, so after 11:00 p.m. you have to use the kerosene lamps.

In the lobby and dining room are huge fireplaces, and that night we sat around while a young man with a guitar played and sang. He asked for requests, and all I could think of was "Celito Lindo" and "Blue Spanish Eyes."

The piggy-backers had left by then, so we were the only guests, apart from two young Mexican fellows from Los Mochis, who were staying there overnight. We befriended them and got along famously, even though they knew only a few words of English (the staff knew even less). Carlos and Hector sat at the table with us for meals, and we taught them English and they taught us Spanish. We had a great time and lots of laughs. We parted good friends, exchanging addresses and promising to write.

The next day we returned to Los Mochis and picked up our little dog Freddie at the hotel. The girl in the travel agency had insisted on taking him to her home overnight. She brought him back to the hotel next day. We tried to pay her for keeping him, but she said, "Gracious, no, I enjoyed it very much. Freddie's my friend!"

The following day we drove to Guaymas, spent the night and then went on to Phoenix. The border town of Nogales is a far cry from San Luis and seemed quite organized.

We made one more trip to Mexico, a few years later, again driving all the way. And I have to say I have enjoyed every moment I've been in that country. At this point I'm going to backtrack a little to the year 1987:

A New Lifestyle

By 1987, Gordon and I had decided we were both ready for a change. We made the move to Vancouver Island; sold our house in Whitehorse and bought one in Saltair; about three miles south of Ladysmith. Gordon's health was slowly deteriorating by this time, due to a series of mini-strokes that hit him, an after-effect of the major one he suffered in July of 1981.

The longer I lived on Vancouver Island the more I fell in love with it. Previously on our rare visits, usually on the way to the desert, I had marveled at the abundance of huge trees and lush foliage, being used to the much smaller variety up north. There was such a profusion of different species of flowers and neatly manicured lawns and shrubs. It made me wonder why we used to hurry to get down to the comparatively arid desert, when all this greenery was available right here. I had always visualized what it would be like to live by the ocean, and now the reality of it was a thrilling thing for me. It truly was a complete change from the wild beauty of the Yukon, which has so many wonders of its own to offer, with the rugged snow-capped mountains and wilderness lakes. It will always have a place in my heart and I still call it "home" when I'm referring to my life up there.

Kirk and Gunn were living on the island in Duncan, B.C., at this time, and we all continued to go back North to the gold mine on Gold Bottom Creek in the Dawson area. It bothered Gordon that he could no longer be of much help with the actual mining. I was kept busy each day cooking for the men and cleaning gold in the evenings.

Kirk finally decided to embark on a new adventure—diamond mining in Venezuela. A longtime friend of his had been down there for the past year on and off, negotiating on a placer gold and diamond concession, which is the equivalent of a claim in our country. He completed all the necessary legal work, permits, etc., and phoned Kirk to see if he would be interested in supplying some equipment and going in partners with him. Kirk flew down there, looked it over carefully, and decided to put our mining claims in Dawson on hold and give it a try.

He hauled one of his Cats (a D-8) and his service truck with welder, tools, etc., to Vancouver and shipped them from there on a freighter that was leaving for Venezuela. Then he drove his pickup to Texas, taking a couple of other fellows along, and they flew from there to Caracas, where they were to meet up with Ken (his partner), and go on out to the concession.

This left Gordon restless and at loose ends. We made the decision that we would make a trip to Florida. Gunn (Kirk's wife) would take the plane from Victoria, meet Gordon in Miami and both of them would fly from there to Caracas. Kirk would meet them at the airport and take them to the mine, which was about twenty-five miles from Santa Elena, the closest town. I had decided to stay with our son Ted and his wife, who were living in Sarasota at the time, until Gordon returned.

A week later we were on our way by car. I did most of the driving between cities, and we traveled 3,600 miles to get there. Ted, his wife, and their six-year-old daughter Helena were living there then, and they had formed a company called Safari-Cam, which produced personalized video films for fishermen featuring their deep-sea fishing adventures. Ted is a photographer. He has produced documentary films and participated in the shooting of movies. He also has experience in underwater photography, having helped produce the film *Pirates of the Deep*, featuring the great white sharks in Australia.

I had the car all to myself in Sarasota, so I could get around and see things on my own when Ted was busy working. The beach was only a fifteen-minute drive from the house, so I spent a lot of time there on the wonderful soft white sand and in the warm ocean. I had to bring some of that sand back in a jar, it feels like talcum powder. I loved everything about Florida, except the extreme humidity at that time of the year. Of course, you don't notice the humidity so much on the beach, which is bordered by tall grass they call sea oats and beautiful red-colored bushes that look like massive foxtail. Arched over the grassy strip at intervals, are beach entrances; walkways of weathered cedar, stretch from the parking lot across the sand to the beach. Some of the beaches have outdoor showers installed, so you can wash the sand off your feet before going back to your car.

I was hoping to see a real thunder and lightning storm while I was there, but all I saw was blue skies, gorgeous sunsets and strange tropical birds that walked with me on the beach. And when you get enough of all that nature stuff (which I never really do!) they have some pretty fantastic malls, too...

It was good to have Gordon back from Venezuela safe and sound. He had really enjoyed it there, but I was anxious, as I hadn't heard a word from him the whole time. Apparently it is quite a drive from the mining camp to a phone. They are way out in bush country. The gold and diamond mining concession the boys picked up there looked promising, he said, but it would take more reading of the ground before they would know the long-term picture. They all really liked it there and were quite comfortable in their air-conditioned trailers.

Ted and I drove the 250 miles to Miami to pick him up at the airport, and on the way home, we took a different route back. Here we noticed airboat rides advertised along the Everglades, so we took the time to investigate. Within minutes we were skimming over and through the tall grass, leaving watery pathways in our wake, as the warm wind whipped through our hair. We hung on for dear life as the driver careened around in circles, sending flocks of startled tropical birds into the sky and finally slowing down so we could watch for alligators lurking in the grass. I had the feeling we were hundreds of miles from civilization of any kind while we were sailing along over those vast Everglades. It was great fun, even though we never saw any alligators...at least, not then!

Later though, on the way home, Ted spotted three very large ones in the canal that ran alongside the road. We stopped and got out of the car, while they just lay there motionless, like logs. You could almost imagine them to be dead, until you saw those big yellow eyes blink occasionally. Apparently they can move very fast, and Ted wouldn't let me get as close as I wanted to, but he did take a picture of me pointing to them. Seeing an alligator in the wild is very different than watching one of them in captivity.

On November 6, Gordon and I left Florida and started out for our old stomping grounds in the desert near Palm Springs. This was a different route from the earlier one. We traveled 2,400 miles in five days, so we didn't spend much time out of the car.

We drove through Louisiana, real Bayou country, miles of swamps with big trees growing in them. Huge bridges have been built up on pillars going over the swamps. Cajun food was advertised everywhere. There were many, many huge industrial plants producing synthetics and plastics; there were also sulfur industries (you can smell sulfur all over) and oil refineries. We got to "Lake Charles" after dark, and it looked like a massive fairy wonderland with all the mills lit up with millions of lights like sparkling castles against the night sky.

On our way to Florida in the car, we had driven through Mississippi. I thought it was a very interesting state. Scattered banyan trees and ivy grew everywhere. Ivy is the ground cover there instead of grass, and you even see it growing up along telephone wires. Long columns of Spanish moss hang from the trees, from about ten feet up right down to the ground. There were big, old Southern country homes with round white pillars and lots of lean, young men in straw hats and coveralls lounging on the banks of streams, fishing for catfish.

So many of the words on the billboards along the roads reminded me of songs from my childhood that my mother used to sing, like "Swanee River," "Dixieland," "Ole Man River," " Citronella," etc. Why my mother, who came from England, used to sing these songs in the Yukon is something of a mystery, but there it is!

But back again to our homeward trip. Going across Texas, we stayed overnight at the "Junction." It looked to us like hunting was the only industry in this small town. The people were curious and friendly, with thick Texas accents. Two local bars were located side by side, so we stopped to have a beer at one of them, where a little group of men was standing around a homemade barrel barbeque outside, joking and drinking beer while one of them tended the meat. The tantalizing aroma wafting over the air was so tempting. Inside the bar, four little kids were amusing themselves at the pool table, while a couple of ladies in jeans and boots weaved between the tables of beer drinkers, with bowls of food they were taking to a table set up at one end of the bar. They were loading it with potato salad, condiments, buns, pumpkin bread and baked beans, family style. In a little while the men began to bring in platters of what turned out to be wild turkey, chicken, goat and beef brisket.

I asked the waitress if we were intruding on a local celebration, and she replied, "Not at all. We do this for all our customers every Sunday. Y'all just grab a plate and dig in with the rest of us, honey! There's no charge." The food was delicious.

The Junction is a very laid-back and quiet little town with just a handful of small businesses, including saddle and boot repair shops. There were a few RVs and campers down by the river, where ducks and geese swam around looking for treats. We enjoyed our reprieve from driving there for a few hours.

When we got to Houston, we just drove on through. Not impressive, it was just another concrete jungle, in that area anyway, with huge modern glass buildings. San Antonio, Texas, was a larger concrete jungle. You had to be impressed though, with the giant maze of overpasses and turnpikes and the ultramodern architectural design of the industrial buildings. One of them in particular, which dominated the horizon, was a massive structure, built entirely of blue glass; the only adornment gracing the exterior was the name; placed very high at the top of the building. It said simply, "Bank One."

Quite a few of our Canadian friends were in Desert Hot Springs already. We stayed there for almost a month; then it was another 1,300-mile drive home. All told, we had driven 13,000 miles since leaving the Island.

Dixie and Lloyd

Our very dear and close friends from Napa, California, Dixie and Lloyd Hall used to come and housesit for us in Saltair, B.C., while we were away mining in the Yukon. They looked after the house and my prized hanging baskets of flowers. Lloyd proceeded to get acquainted with all the neighbors there and knew more about the area than we did by the time we came back. They kept the house and lawn immaculate, and it was such a treat to come home to this in the fall.

These two had become like family to us over the years. It was on one of our winter trips to Desert Hot Springs in California that we first met. We hit it off immediately, and Lloyd became fascinated with the stories that Gordon told about our mining adventures up north. They decided to come up one summer and see the country for themselves. They drove all the way from Napa, California, to see us in Atlin, B.C. when we were working our first mining claims.

Totally self-contained in their truck and camper, they watched our mining operation with great interest, helping out in any way they could. A year later we had moved to Mount Freegold in the Carmacks area, and one day who should unexpectedly arrive but Dixie and Lloyd. And, true to form, when we began mining our final and last creek on Gold Bottom in Dawson, they visited again.

We had met these folks during the years that Gordon and I still had our home in Whitehorse. At that time we used to spend several months each winter in the desert, with our own motor vehicle. The mining season only lasted about four months, so we went south with the rest of the "snowbirds" from Canada for about three months. As a rule, we stopped by to see Dixie and Lloyd in Napa along the way. They loved showing us the sights there, and several times they took us on a wine-tasting tour where we got to sample the excellent wines for which that area is famous. We would buy one of the recommended brands, then stop at a deli for cheese and fresh bread to take to their favorite park, where we would stop and have a picnic.

They joined us in Desert Hot Springs a little later and booked into a Mobile Home Park very close to the one where we always stayed. All the mobile parks in that area have naturally heated pools. There is a comparatively small pool for those who like it hot and a larger one for swimming, that actually has to be cooled off, because the natural hot springs are far too hot to use otherwise. This is one of the advantages of staying there, instead of across the highway in Palm Springs where the pools have to be heated.

6

Second Trip to Florida and My First to Venezuela

We left Nanaimo in November, 1994, and drove to Desert Hot Springs, where we had our trailer stored. Our ultimate destination was Venezuela, to visit our son Kirk who was mining there. We boarded a plane from Palm Springs to Florida, with our friend Charlie, who had decided to come along with us on this trip. He had a daughter he wanted to visit, who lived close to Sarasota, where our son Ted and his wife Irena had their home.

Ted met us at the Tampa Airport and we dropped Charlie off along the way. Irena and their little girl, Helena, were at home to greet us. Irena's mom and dad, along with her sister, Stella, were there too, so we got to meet them for the first time. We all had a very pleasant Christmas together.

Ted drove us to Tampa on January 10, where we met Charlie again at the airport and flew via American Airlines to Miami. There, we transferred to Servivensa Airlines and went on to Caracas, where Kirk was waiting for us.

He met us at the airport, and we went to the hotel he was staying at, about forty-five minutes away by taxi. It was dark by then, so we got to see the city at night. It seemed smoky, smoggy and crowded to me, and the fumes going through all the tunnels stung my eyes. The hotel was okay, though, and we had a good visit over dinner.

We made the drive the next morning back to the airport by taxi. In the daylight, Caracas looked interesting. I would have liked to explore a little, but we had a plane to catch to Cuidad Bolivar. A friend, Benny, met us there with Kirk's red Toyota pickup; he had it shining like a jewel inside and out. Again we booked into a hotel and Charlie, Gordon and I looked around town a bit while Kirk and Benny drove around picking up camp supplies and attending to some company business. That evening we took a small tour of the city. I liked it a lot better than Caracas. We had dinner and walked down by the river. The air was balmy, and the folks strolling along the boardwalk seemed so relaxed and friendly. I decided I was going to like Venezuela.

The following day Kirk planned on driving the pickup to Santa Elena (the closest town to the mine). He put Charlie, Gordon and me on a small ten-passenger plane. We arrived in the midmorning, and there at the airport to meet us were Floyd and Esther, and Erich, as they call him there. I was quite surprised that they seemed to know us already. The truth came out in the next few minutes that they had all read my book, so we were greeted almost like old friends.

Esther said Kirk had told her to take us out to the "plantation" (they called it Kirk's Place) but that we could stay with her if we would rather. Erich said we were most welcome to stay at his place as guests, he also had rooms for rent, but we opted for the plantation, thinking that Kirk would be back by the next morning. Erich had lived in the Yukon for a while, but now he lived in Santa Elena, where he and his pretty young South American wife ran a boarding house and dining room for their guests.

Esther was a tall, attractive dark-haired lady, very much in charge of any situation that might come up. She had taken on the job of showing newly arrived prospectors and businessmen around, explaining the customs of the people and sometimes acting as an interpreter as well. She even did the negotiating for those traveling to Brazil, at the customs office. Her husband, Floyd, had a diamond concession of his own. Kirk and Gunn had become her close friends, on their first trip to Santa Elena.

After taking us to her home first, and showing us around town, she drove us out to Kirk's. She was as surprised as we were to see that the only things at all in that big house were two mattresses on the floor. No sheets, blankets, towels, toilet paper—nothing except for a bedspread on one of the mattresses! So she went home, gathered up some sheets and towels and the basic necessities.

Apparently the motels in that town aren't the greatest, and we preferred to stay where we were at the plantation anyway. The grounds outside were wonderful, a real tropical paradise, with eight varieties of fruit palms: oranges, limes, grapefruit, passionfruit, grenadilla, guava, papaya, mango and lemons. They also had coffee beans growing there, cashew nuts and peppers among other things. There was about five acres of ground, but being vacant for quite a while, it needed a lot of work and attention, so Kirk had plans for a live-in caretaker for a while to get the place in shape again.

"I'll pick you up at six, and we'll go for dinner," Esther said. "You'll need some rest now." It turned out that Kirk and Benny had to wait two more days in Cuidad Bolivar for some parts that hadn't shown up yet. The plans were for us to go out to the mining camp when they got back, so we made do with what we had at the plantation until then. We had four bathrooms with showers (hardly any pressure, however) and electricity. With Esther there to pick us up for meals and take us to a café, showing us the sights in the meantime, we did just fine.

Gradually, we got to roam around town a bit on our own, although Gordon's legs couldn't stand too much mileage. He had hoped there would be an extra pickup or jeep available, but there was a definite shortage of transportation vehicles. It seemed to me as if the "investor" could have bought one less excavator from Ritchie Bros. and a couple of extra pickups for camp.

Two days in a row, Esther went over to Erich's and borrowed his van to take us around on a sightseeing tour. We met some of her family out in the country, two brothers and her father, who was celebrating his eightieth birthday the first day. We had coffee and a cake that Esther had brought along, and listened to the old man's stories. He came from Scotland originally; moved to South America and raised his family in Guiana, where they lived until they were forced to leave, during a government coup.

Floyd was also in Guiana at that time and luckily managed to get away in his own plane, even though the army refused to let him leave the country. He left behind more than a million dollars worth of assets when he slipped away, guns shooting at his aircraft as he took off. Floyd's home used to be in Texas, before that. His ex-wife and family were still living there.

Esther showed us the waterfalls and the beautiful San Cabana mountain country on a perfect day when the peaks were free of clouds and mist. We took her two girls and Erich's four boys with us, and they rode in the back of the van with Charlie and Esther's sister-in-law. Charlie fell in love that day, but that's another story…

Erich's boys were rather undisciplined and noisy, but after the first fifteen minutes the girls had them all organized, and they entertained us all the rest of the way with songs they had learned in school. Some of them were even in English, and they were the same nursery rhymes I had also learned at that age. They sang in unison, and their voices were lovely.

One day Bill, Kirk's manager, and his wife Linda came from the mining camp to do some shopping, so Esther took us all across the border to Brazil. We had two vehicles that day, as they wanted to buy some things to take back to camp. Esther did all the negotiating in the stores for Bill, as she was familiar with the currency.

When we came to the border she gathered up all our passports and took them into the office, where she handed them over to the customs officer. I was rather alarmed when she came back out and said we would pick them up again on the way home. But she seemed to know them very well in the office, and apparently that happens quite regularly.

Next, we went to a café and had a barbeque and some very good Brazilian beer. A dark-skinned man cooked the meat—beef, pork and chicken—outside on a long skewer, then brought it to our table and carved it right onto our plate. There was a steam table where we could help ourselves to side dishes, like beans, stewed tomatoes and farina, which, I was told, is the ground-up root of the farina tree. It has the texture of corn meal. They serve it almost dry, and it has a nutty flavor. It had little rolled-up balls of ham in it, which I found out later was smoked snake meat. Anyway, it was very tasty.

Crude mining equipment.

All the stores in that town were exceptionally neat and well organized. They seemed to specialize in gorgeous hand loomed hammocks, in a large assortment of colors.

Our favorite eating place in Santa Elena was "El Quiote," just on the edge of town, a few minutes walk from Esther and Floyd's home. I will miss forever the wonderful fresh-squeezed fruit juices, served in large frosted milkshake glasses, still frothy from the blender and ice cold. What a variety! You could order it natural or sweetened, pineapple, orange, apple, guava, papaya, passion fruit, watermelon or a mixture of the above. The restrooms were spotless and actually had soap, and the staff was friendly and went all out for the Canadians. We noticed there seemed to be a lot of good will toward Canadians in Santa Elena.

Kirk and Benny arrived home from Cuidad Bolivar finally, and Kirk took us to see all the new equipment stored at the ritzy country club just out of town. The owners, a Venezuelan family, had loaned him a remote control key to the huge, carved ironwood gate. It slid open and we drove to the far end of the property. A big garage, almost like an airplane hangar, was Benny's hangout. He leased this part of the property from the owners, so he could use it to work on the two helicopters he was rebuilding for his own use. One end of the building was his living quarters—very neat and well kept. He bought and hauled all his furniture over from Brazil. The Brazilian border is only a twenty-mile drive from Santa Elena. The furniture was massive and heavy. They call the wood Angelina Padre. It comes from the ironwood tree, the hardest wood known to man, and has a beautiful red color and a luster much like rosewood. (Kirk planned on furnishing his whole house out at the Plantation from this same wood. We were a week too early!)

Benny's office desk was made of this wood also, and he proudly showed us his new acquisitions, a new computer and fax machine. Just outside his living quarters, and on the edge of the clearing, there was a windmill built over a deep well. There the property dropped off into a ravine, with very tall palm trees. At the base of the trees a spring formed a deep pool, which Benny planned on converting into a swimming hole.

The recent shipment of equipment was lined up outside the garage, over a million dollars worth of clean, rebuilt D-8 Cats

Later developments.

and huge excavators, compressors and so on. They were all to be moved out to the mining camp in the next few days. One important function of all that equipment was to reforest the land as the mining proceeded and leave everything in perfect condition before moving to various locations. I took pictures of everything, then we went back to town and had dinner. We noticed right away that everyone in Santa Elena seemed to know Kirk. He couldn't drive through town without being stopped by a dozen people, wanting to talk and shake hands. He conversed with them quite well by then, although we didn't have a clue what they were talking about.

A couple of days later Kirk took us out to the mining camp, a three-hour drive over a very rough dirt road. We winched ourselves out of one deep mud hole and helped a couple of other travelers as well. The mining camp was in the heart of the jungle. The men had cleared an area and set up a couple of fairly new house trailers. Bill, the camp manager, and his wife Linda, the cook, used one. Both trailers had air conditioning. The second one was the temporary cook trailer, with a bedroom and bathroom on the end, which Kirk and Gunn used when they were there. Kirk turned his bedroom over to Gordon and I for our stay, and he stayed in one of the five new cabins they built for the crew. Charlie had the use of one of the cabins also, as most of the crew hadn't arrived back from Christmas holidays yet. A long table with benches was set up on a cement pad alongside the cook trailer for serving meals outside.

We had arrived at the Dos Cerros mining camp, at last. This was the main reason for the trip in the first place, to see Kirk and his mining operation.

The wheels of progress turn much, much slower in Venezuela than in our country. Obtaining government permits for everything, including shipping supplies and parts into the country, can take months to complete. Crossing all the hurdles involved and dealing with miles of red tape, plus learning the regulations of a foreign country is very time consuming. It had taken over a year and a half, but the camp was very close to being setup in a first-class manner. The equipment was there and the whole operation would be in production very shortly. We were maybe two weeks too early to see the new plant in full operation, but in the meantime the hand miners had been carrying on in their usual manner, and the proceeds (in diamonds) from their efforts helped a lot to pay current expenses.

Yes! We found some.

93

A hot chicken dinner was waiting for us when we arrived. It was almost dark by now, and we were hungry. While we were sitting around the table outside the trailers, a tawny little wild cat showed up. (I thought it was a baby leopard because of its spots.) Tigra was six-months old, a delightful playful animal, loved by everyone there, even though she played a bit rough at times. She would leap onto my shoulders and try to nibble my neck. She had been there since she was small enough to fit into the palm of your hand. She stayed around camp most of the day, but always, when nightfall came, she became wild again slipped away into the jungle to hunt, even though she got lots of cooked chicken and other good food at camp. I took a whole roll of film that first day.

When I was a kid, just learning to read, my very favorite books were the *Jungle Books*, by Rudyard Kipling. "Mowgli" and I were close companions in my imagination, and the wild animals of the jungle were our best friends. It was in the middle of the night, when the light plant was turned off, that the full significance of it hit me—"God, here I am out here in the real jungle!" Laying there in the darkness of the house-trailer, there were only window screens between us and a myriad of strange, unfamiliar night sounds. There was a whole orchestration of weird and wonderful voices out there, and I was hearing it for the very first time. I sat up and looked out the window, too euphoric to sleep. This was the real thing! The stars even seemed brighter up

Tigra

94

Joyce with Ocelot "Tigra

there. My eyes were startled back to earth by little darting lights. At first I thought they must be the eyes of small animals glowing in the dark, but as I watched them swaying gracefully, twinkling off and on, I realized that they must be fireflies. I watched the haunting, mysterious lights for a long time, wondering what they looked like in the daylight. I found out later that some of them are little blue butterflies. I listened to the night murmurs until the sounds became familiar and then drifted off into a peaceful sleep.

The next day the hand miners (about a mile down the trail) notified Kirk that they were going to have a cleanup, so Charlie, Gordon and I went along to watch. It was quite fascinating to see the procedure in person, even though we had seen it on video previously. They ended up this day with seven carats of diamonds. It had taken several days of sluicing to produce this amount. Later, Kirk took them to the office in Oteros camp (a mile up the trail in the opposite direction), and I watched while Michael (Oteros' bookkeeper) weighed and locked them away in a safe.

Some more of the crew had arrived back in Santa Elena, and a day later Kirk had to go back there to get them started putting the blades back on the new Cats and getting the equipment ready for moving out to camp.

95

"I'll be back tonight or tomorrow morning," he said. We didn't really think he could make it that soon. There was so much to attend to and so many demands on his time that I don't know how he handled it all.

That day I came down with a form of the flu (although we'd had flu shots before we left home). For a couple of days I was pretty much out of it-fever, cough, the runs, the works. Then suddenly the fever left as quickly as it had come, and a good thing, too, because Gordon came down with it next, only twenty times worse. By this time the rest of the crew was at camp, Greg and Paul had taken the only extra pickup into town. This left Gordon and I, Charlie and the cook, and her husband, Bill, at camp. Kirk still hadn't arrived, and we had no communication with town and no transportation of any kind.

The next two days were a nightmare. On the third day some people came through on motorcycles, and we managed to send a message to town with them for a helicopter to come and pick us up, but unknown to us the only chopper in Santa Elena had the motor out for repairs.

Gordon refused to eat, drink or take any pills. He just lay there, burning up with fever, too weak to get out of bed. I spent all my time in the room with him giving him sponge baths, trying to get some water down him and changing and rinsing out underwear by hand.

Linda, all during this time, was ignoring the situation and me entirely. Bill was working on the sewer pipes, trying to get them hooked up, and Charlie was busy trying to dazzle Linda with his charm and wit. Another day dragged on, and at one point I managed to get a 282 into Gordon and an hour later his fever broke. He thought he could manage some toast and coffee. An hour later he had lost it, and the fever was back with a vengeance. Next day, same thing—aspirin and sponge baths broke the fever for a while then back it came worse than before. The diarrhea pills had worked by now, so I thought at least that part was over.

I never knew just how, but someone got the message to Kirk (in Santa Elena) that his dad was sick. I guess the helicopter man must have told him; anyway, Norm Pierson, Gary and Paul (part of the crew) arrived from town one evening with the pickup. They said they were going back in the morning and Kirk wanted us to go in with them. I said, "Forget it, there's no way he'll go in over that road and survive. We'll have to wait for a helicopter."

Bill went in with them the next day, and they promised to send a helicopter the next morning. All the next day we waited. Nothing. By this time my nerves were frayed so badly I was a wreck. Gordon's fever had returned for the third time, just before Bill left for town, and I had broken down in tears.

"Just get a chopper out here, please, and don't tell Kirk how sick his dad is, he has got enough on his mind. I'll just charter a plane and get him home. It's my fault for letting him come here in the first place. Don't let Kirk know I'm upset." I implored him, almost totally irrational. Linda had just turned her back and walked away, like she always did whenever I showed up.

That evening was the turning point for Gordon. The fever left, he got up and washed and had a bite to eat. But he looked terribly haggard. Later that evening Kirk arrived from town with one pickup and Bill the other. We learned about the helicopter, and as Gordon was feeling much better, decided we would take him in by pickup in the morning.

My farewell to Linda the next day was, "Thanks for everything, Linda. It's been real fun." She didn't bother waving. Bill took Charlie in his truck as he had to go in for more food, and Kirk, Gordon and I went in the other, driving very carefully.

Kirk with Diamonds

When we got to Santa Elena, Gordon seemed very tired, so we put him to bed on the mattress at the plantation. He said he would be fine, so Kirk suggested I go with him to watch the transaction when he sold some diamonds. We were gone about an hour and a half when I thought I had better get back and see how Gordon was. We picked up some fresh, cold drinking water and Kirk dropped me off at the door, as he had some more running around to do.

The minute I walked in I knew something was wrong. The smell was awful. He had tried to get up off the mattress and go to the bathroom, but the extreme exertion of trying to push himself off the floor just emptied his bowels totally and suddenly. Not realizing the extent of the accident, I helped pull him onto his feet and into the bathroom. I got him seated on the toilet with his trousers and shorts in a heap around his feet and went to look for a plastic bag in the kitchen. Luckily I found one and ran back with it, only to find he had tried to clean himself up with toilet tissue. He hadn't noticed it was all over his hands and he had touched his shirt and face. The toilet bowl itself was covered. Somehow in my agitation I had stepped in it, and my shoes were making mucky tracks wherever I walked. I had only half of a roll of paper to clean this all up with. No rags, no mop, no laundry facilities, nothing. In the muggy heat of the afternoon, sweat was pouring down my face, my head was pounding, chest hurting and I was crying with stress and frustration.

Gordon just sat there, helpless, too weak to move. I walked to the bedroom door, took my shoes off, grabbed a clean white sock out of the suitcase for a washcloth, and a clean white T-shirt for a mopping rag. Back to the bathroom, I put my dirty shoes on again and turned on the shower. The faucet was faulty and wouldn't spray, just dribbled out cold water. I managed to get him in the shower, where I held him up with one hand (he couldn't stand alone and didn't even complain about the cold water). I mopped him down with soap and my white sock, dried him with our only towel and somehow got him dressed and back into bed, clean and dry.

He immediately dropped into a deep sleep. Shaking like a leaf, I went back into the bathroom for the big clean-up job. With his white T-shirt, I started mopping up, rinsing it in the toilet and waiting for the bowl to fill up again (slowly) before I could do anymore. I threw his shorts into the garbage bag and debated about doing the same to his trousers, but he had only brought two pairs along, so I got the bulk of it off in the toilet and threw them on the floor.

In the midst of all this hell, Kirk came back and found me there. He took right over. (Thank God for sons, I really needed one right then.) He found a mop and plastic pail somewhere, there was a faucet outside with good water pressure that I didn't know about, and began throwing buckets of water over the floor. It ran into the shower and down the drain. Then he put Gordon's clothes in the bucket to soak and went off to get some cold drinking water, paper towels, etc. "You get some rest, Mom, and don't worry, he'll be okay now."

When Kirk left I collapsed in a little heap on the foot of the mattress. I was sorry we had come and put this extra burden on him at a time like this. The exhaustion was overwhelming. Wiping the sweat and tears from my face, I thought, "What would I do if this happened on the way home, in the plane or even the car?" I felt old, defeated and hopeless. I don't think anyone thought Gordon would make it through that day, but at least he lay clean and warm and asleep for a while.

It must have been about an hour later, when I woke up. For a while I couldn't remember where we were. I was only aware of Gordon's even breathing, then the other sounds flooded my consciousness—the healing, peaceful sounds of crickets and birds and chickens in the distance and the rustling of palm fronds in the breeze outside the open window. My whole body was heavy with relaxation, and I just lay there a while longer, not wanting to think or move a muscle. After awhile a little ray of hope appeared.

"This isn't the end of the world," I thought. "We've survived tougher times than this. We're going to beat this thing and enjoy what is left of this trip! It isn't everybody who gets to check out the diamond mines in the jungles of South America, especially at our ages..."

Kirk came back a little later. He had been to the hospital and brought two bottles of the liquid they give people intravenously to prevent dehydration and build up one's system. He also brought some special diarrhea pills. By eight o'clock that evening Gordon was strong enough to get up and go over to Esther's with us. She had cooked up some special plantain soup for him, and he ate that with some fresh baked bread. Then Kirk helped him stand up and walk to the pickup to go home.

After that, Gordon managed to snap back quite well. We even had a going-away party out at the country club with barbequed fish and fabulous cheeses and drinks. We played dominoes with the host, who didn't want us to leave and kept bringing on more trays of food and delicacies, whenever we tried to go home. I worried that we would miss the plane the next morning, because as we finally left with Frank (who was driving us home), our host had a death grip on Kirk's arm, and wasn't letting him leave yet, even if it meant knocking him over the head. We had a good time, and, with Frank acting as interpreter, our friend declared that his home was ours. His food, dog, money, everything he had was ours anytime we came to Santa Elena.

Erich very kindly offered us one of his charter planes to fly directly from Santa Elena to Caracas, so we could leave the same day we had to catch our plane there to Miami. It made our trip back to Florida much easier.

7

Lara's Home

We sat around her small livingroom, a group of strangers, yet we all seemed compatible, drawn together by some invisible force. The mere presence of Lara can lift your spirit the moment you enter her home. She simply greeted us with a warm hug and radiant smile and made sure we were comfortable. We sat quietly until, one by one, her guests began to communicate their various concerns and feelings. No one was pressured to participate; all were free to either talk or listen with no one judging or criticizing.

Lying on a couch was an old man, almost wasted away and dying of cancer. His wife was sitting beside him, so was Lara's friend, Grace, who was holding the man's hand in hers and talking to him in a soothing tone. He was almost asleep, with a peaceful happy expression on his face. After awhile, he and his wife stood up to leave. Lara, with an arm around each, walked them to the door. "Come whenever you wish," she told them. "Come soon!"

She asked my husband, Gordon, about his recent stroke and had him lie on the floor face down, while she massaged his neck and back. I leaned back in my chair and thought about events of the past few months, reliving the horror of that day when the blow had been dealt and desperately hoping Lara could help him to accept it. What I would have given to just erase the past year and start all over again. Maybe she could help him realize that he deserved to relax now, instead of feeling so much anger. Maybe he wasn't as productive as he was in the past, but he's paid his dues, I thought.

Now Lara was talking to me. "This is where all the anger

builds up and causes tension," she said, indicating the back of his neck and shoulders. I had always suspected that the stroke was partly due to his attitude—taking things too seriously and worrying all the time. He realized it himself but couldn't seem to do a thing about it. I looked into her eyes, startled, because it was as though she had been reading my mind. This incredible person, who was seeing us for the first time, not only knew exactly what I was feeling but also sensed what Gordon's problem was!

Tears that must have been dammed up for a long time suddenly welled up in my eyes, and I when I tried to choke them back, Grace stood up and led me into a room at the end of the house before anyone noticed. She put her arms around me, and suddenly I was sobbing out all the pain and hurt of the last few months.

"That's good," she said. "You needed to do that; you'll feel much better now." When we joined the others again, Gordon was back in his easy chair, and Lara was reading aloud a poem she had written. I was thrilled when she gave me a copy later on. I noticed she hadn't signed it, but she just shrugged.

"How can I take credit when the words just flow through me from somewhere else? I just write them down."

She had "opened her home" on Thursday afternoons to anyone who cared to come. She did this for no personal gain except for the spiritual satisfaction that the healing brought her. When we left her that day, we drove home in a glow of warmth and well being that stayed with us a long time.

Gordon was receiving professional home therapy at the time, but I believe the several visits we made to Lara's house helped him a lot. Unfortunately, he decided against any kind of therapy soon after that and would not be persuaded.

Here is Lara's poem. (The names in this episode have been changed by request, and the poem is the property of the author.)

The Path of Silence

Today I entered into the path of darkness
The deepest seat of the abyss,
With all my defenses down.
Let the Ego shoot his poison.

I will stand and walk
Without being proud,
Without importance,
Without any fear.
Sending beaming lights of love
Into the darkness,
Without being recognized or rewarded.
Just to Be...
That's survival;
Not beans and rice in the cupboards.
A clear mind and an empty body;
A pulsing heart
Which will never cease or stop.
Feet steady, anchored in the earth,
Inhaling the warmth from the mother
Who gave matter to me
As a base of my existence.
All that is concealed will emerge at last.
I want it too, it's my choice.
It will always Be, I will always Be.
Never die, never cease.
Beginning and end
Joining in the circle of the flow.
Infinitely.
Finally I'm waking—waking up to myself.
Me who slept for eons—
Me who will wake forever.
My yes will be yes.
My no will be no.
Firm—never in between.
Hands who talk the language of my home,
My home in the flow, the flow of love.
The love which supports everything
Without expectation, without spite.
I entered the darkness today,
The cold flames of hell
Threaten to consume me.
But I keep on walking until I reach the door
Which conceals the light.

And the light puts an end to the darkness.
Now I walk, strong and flexible.
No panic in my stomach,
No faltering in my words;
No fluttering in my heart,
All is firm and calm.
And the river of life, born out of love,
Flows, touches and heals all my wounds.
Wounds from the cross, and the long journey.
Bleed and burn; the light is near.
My head straight up in the sky,
Which had locked her stars away.
I am alone, but I have found Me.
Walk, walk; let your tears be your comfort;
Until they transform into diamonds,
Jewels...forever casting colors
Into the darkness.
I am exceeding myself.
I am born.
I AM

— *by* A FRIEND

My Life on the Internet

There was a period in my life, when much of my time was taken up with a group of people on the internet. It seemed at that time they were my only social life, as I was confined to the house so much. These were people who had formed a storytelling website where "members only" were allowed. It grew rapidly, though, through word of mouth. It was run by a man we called Uncle Timmie, who, as webmaster for the group, held high standards for his little flock of followers. In appreciation for the time and effort he put in, contributing himself to the stories and publishing them in the "Attic," as we called our website, he expected all of us to do our share in submitting written material almost daily.

Most of our members wrote about their own lives and experiences, so it was inevitable that we became quite close, like a family, after a year or so. And the Attic grew by leaps and

Network noshing

Tim and family.

Nerdnosh' is a virtual campfire

bounds, much to Timmie's great delight. This became my social outlet during the time I had to be alone so much as caregiver for my late husband.

As it turned out, my designation (bestowed upon me by our leader) was to talk for wolf. I enquired just what that meant. It appears that there is an American frontier fable that goes like this: "The Anasazi came to a new home. The rivers ran deep and clear all year round and the soil was rich, and game filled the woods. However, there were many wolves. They determined to kill the wolves. Then they thought again of it. They did not want to be the people who killed the wolves.

"They realized that summer turned to fall and the spring and the years came and went. The problem of the wolves would come again and again to them. That is why they designated one of their number always to appear at the council fires. To Talk For Wolf."

Eventually though, after a year or two, the inevitable happened, one by one members seemed to be dropping out of the circle. And, reluctantly, I did the same, as it was taking up too much of my time. Several of us kept in touch for a few years, but gradually drifted apart. I still think of the good times we all had together, though, and often wonder where and how they all are.

When I first joined "Nernosh," as it was called, they had been having face-to-face get-togethers or "Noshcoms", in different

105

areas of the world, and those who could afford the time and money, met for these gatherings once a year.

One summer I talked my granddaughter, Tanja, into joining me for a trip to San Francisco for my first Noshcom with the group. She wasn't a member, but came along as a guest. Following are some of the notes I wrote back then about our adventure.

Our Trip to San Francisco

Tanja and I arrived at the San Francisco airport at 10:20 p.m. on Tuesday. Both of us had travel bags on wheels that we pulled behind us. They had just squeezed under the limit for size requirements, so we had taken them aboard the plane with us. We checked through customs, then wondered however we were going to find Lee and Donna, the couple who were going to meet us, in this huge terminal. We reasoned that they would probably be at the baggage pickup, which turned out to be at the opposite end of the building. Anticipating a long fast hike, we started off in that direction. In just a few minutes I heard a voice behind me calling, "Joyce!" We had walked right past them. Lee was hold-

Al Capone's cell in Alcatraz.

106

ing a large placard that said, "Joyce and Tanja's Welcoming Committee."

Big hugs all around, and we set out for the town of Pacifica, seventeen miles out of San Francisco, in great spirits, chatting away like magpies as if we had known each other all our lives.

"We'll see you tomorrow around noon," said Lee, and they were off to their hotel in the heart of the city. Tanja and I felt as if we were still up there in the clouds. The feeling lasted during the whole trip.

At the Sea-Breeze Motel in Pacifica, a big motherly woman greeted us as warmly as if we were her long-lost children; she gave us each a key and ensured us that there had never been one case of criminal activity in the area that she had heard of.

The peaceful sound of the waves washing in on the beach seemed to reinforce her observation. In the dark we could see the white froth sweeping over the sand and receding again, and we listened to the rhythm of the sea. Once snuggled in our beds, it lulled us to sleep, and both of us woke in the morning refreshed and impatient to see it all in the daylight.

And what a sight it was! The wind had come up during the night; there wasn't a hint of fog, just clear blue sky and powerful waves crashing against the giant boulders that rose up here and there along the water's edge. A painter's paradise, I thought.

We had a relaxing breakfast in a window nook at Nick's Sea-Breeze Restaurant, returning to our room to find Donna and Lee in their car outside, waiting for us. Lee drove us into the city, where we took in Fisherman's Wharf. I've never seen such a huge attractive display of seafood in my life. We ate yummy fish cakes in a very nice café.

While there, we checked out the time schedule for the Alcatraz Tour and were told that it was booked for the next few days, but they did have four tickets available. We decided right there that we had better grab them. While we were at it Tanja and I purchased tickets for *Phantom of the Opera* as well.

Lee drove us to the St. Peter's Cathedral and asked if we would like to go inside. Did we ever! This was the same place I had written a story about, for the Attic, very recently. Gordon and I had seen this cathedral many years before. (We had almost had a family fight there.) I think Lee must have remembered that

107

story, and being the nice, thoughtful man that he is, made a point of taking us there. It was as impressive as ever, although the pipe organ wasn't playing this time. Here is the story I had written.

Two Points of View

While taking in the sights of San Francisco with our son and his wife, a friend of ours, Frank, offered to show us around, which resulted in a most enjoyable day in that city. Gordon and I belong to no organized religions, believing that all of them have their good and bad points, but one of the most impressive moments that day, I thought, was a visit to Saint Paul's Cathedral.

Once inside, we discovered that we were all alone in this immense place, and we gazed around, mesmerized by the splendor of it all; the domed ceiling seemed to reach to the sky, and hanging on long golden chains were enormous glittering crystal chandeliers. Crimson carpets in the aisles between the pews accented the richness of polished hardwood floors. The crimson was repeated in the velvet drapes with gold tassels, framing the magnificent stained glass windows. Surrounding the pulpit were exquisite sculptures of the Virgin Mary and the Saints, looking down on us.

At first we spoke to each other in whispers, not realizing we were doing it, and even our whispers seemed to echo in that silence. Silence can hold many things. It can be eerie and frightening, peaceful and relaxing, filled with suspense or empty and lonesome. The silence that day in the cathedral was awesome and immense, filled with expectancy and unseen spirits.

Suddenly a door opened way over on the far wall of the church, and a solitary priest appeared. With his head slightly down and palms held together reverently before him, he moved slowly down the aisle, chanting softly. Even so, his rich baritone resonated clearly throughout the building. When he reached the statue of the Virgin Mary he paused, genuflected, then disappeared through another door. We never saw him again, but suddenly the air was reverberating with the deep rich tones of the pipe organ. The glorious sound of music pulsated through the cathedral filling every inch of space...rising up to the ceiling and out beyond, carrying me right along with it.

Frank found his voice first. "Doesn't it give you a warm feeling," he said to me, "to realize that this beautiful building was built by the people, as a token of their love for the Savior?" My heart was so full I couldn't speak. Until a voice behind me sounded in my ear, jolting me unceremoniously back to earth.

"I wonder how many poor peasants had to donate a pig apiece to pay for this spread?" Gordon remarked, casually. Quickly, I looked around, hoping that Frank hadn't heard. Cold, hard reality had no room in the space I was in right then.

Gordon has always had a steadying influence on me. It's interesting to speculate what life would have been without it...

But back to my trip to San Francisco with Timmie and the gang. We drove the most crooked (and steep and narrow) street in the world; we also went up in the Coit Tower, where we marveled at the paintings and the fabulous view of the city. We saw much more that day, before our very competent "tour guides" dropped their most appreciative passengers off at our motel again, with the promise to see us again tomorrow.

"Tim and the rest should be here by then," they said. We offered to rent a car of our own, to save them all the mileage, but they wouldn't hear of it. Tim's brother, Reloj, who is a schoolteacher in Anchorage, Alaska, was to join us as well. He was well known to us all (via the internet) for his wry sense of humor.

Beach in Pacifica, San Francisco.

Beach in Pacifica, San Francisco.

The third morning , I went for an early walk around the village of Pacifica while Tanja sun-tanned on Rockaway Beach. Coming back to our motel room, I decided to get ready for the day ahead so the bathroom would be free for Tanja, when she got back.

I just stepped out of the shower when a knock came at the door. Thinking that my granddaughter must have left her key behind, I ran to the door with a towel around me and my hair dripping wet. I was about to let her in and had the doorknob in my hand when something inside my head said, "Stop!" and I peeked through the closed drapes to see two men standing outside. I recognized them from a picture Tim had sent me a long time ago.

"Oh, my god!" I said to myself (apparently I said it out loud, because Reloj told me later that he heard me). I dove back into the bathroom and yelled, "Come in! I'm just in the bathroom..."

Through the door I heard the words: "How do we know we're in the right room?" Before I could answer, the next question came: "How do you know who we are?"

We carried on like this for a while, laughing and kibitzing through the closed door, until suddenly I realized my clothes were all in the other room. There was only one thing to do.

"Go away and come back in fifteen minutes!" I yelled.

Came the reply, "Well, we've certainly enjoyed the conversation so far..."

A short time later Tanja and I joined them next door in Nick's café, and the hilarity continued. On the table were Reloj's laptop and the Noshcom pig—the mascot we learned was carved by the great "Dean of Pig Carvers." We couldn't have felt more at home with each other.

Lee and Donna joined us before long, and we all went into town and ended up driving up to Tim's place in the country and up a fairly steep, long hill. It was even better than I had envisioned. A magical lush green fairyland of a place to live. And we got to meet the gracious and lovable Nicki J. This was the highlight of the trip for me, the part I will remember the longest. Tanja said later, echoing my feelings exactly, "Grandma, I just wanted to take her home with me!"

Nicki J. made Chai tea for us, a delicious concoction I had never tried before, and brought on a basket of fresh breads and fruit.

I won't try to describe their home, but it is spacious and welcoming with high-beamed ceiling and a rustic stairway leading upstairs to Timmie's Den, where he spends most of his time, and where the Nosh and Klatsch were born and is maintained.

The next day Tanja and I went into San Francisco via taxi. We explored the stores and did a little shopping, then met with the group in a clubroom at David's Deli for the "Gathering Gathering." What fun putting a face to all those personalities— usually it's the other way around. I found myself screaming, "Gene! It's you," and "Tracy, I had imagined you were blonde," and on and on. I think it was the next morning that Lu and JC and Manzie arrived. I had always enjoyed his almost daily comments and stories.

Tanja and I were still in bed, just reminiscing about the previous day when they knocked on the door. It was wonderful to see them. Lu looked exactly how I had her pictured, blonde and demure and smiling with delicate features and very pretty. I had pictured JC as being fair haired, tall, slight and talkative. Instead he had dark, curly hair, was sturdily built and very quiet. (Of course, he was surrounded by four females, so didn't have much

Beach in Pacifica, San Francisco

chance to get a word in.) Manzie has red hair, a little round face and luminous big blue eyes. I wanted to hold her immediately.

She was as good as gold the whole time; in fact, at the campfire Uncle Tim held her on his lap for most of the evening. Long after she had fallen into a contented sleep. It was quite touching to see our fearless leader sitting there on the log, just watching the flames dancing in the fire, and rocking a sleeping child in his arms. (Tragically, a few months later this lovely child drowned in her grandmother's patio pool. The whole Nosh group mourned along with Lu and JC, and tried their best to give them emotional support.)

The campfire was a huge success. We had many toasts to those who couldn't be there for this one. We enjoyed the tour of Alcatraz with Lee and Donna immensely. *Phantom of the Opera* was superb. The Thai dinner in Pacifica that Tanja and I had with Tracy was excellent, as was her company. In fact everything about Noshcom was so enjoyable I didn't want it to end. It was hard to say goodbye to everyone. I'm certain the memories will last forever.

The Book Launch

There's an old Heritage building in Nanaimo that was once the B.C. Telegraph Office. In the summer of 1996 it was, and had been for a long time, a very special little bookstore, called simply, The Bookstore on Bastion Street. The owners were Thora and Jerome Howell, and because of their dedication, hard work and passion for good stories, the place had become famous over the years for its book launches and readings. People here scanned the newspapers eagerly to learn when the next event would be taking place, as Thora hosted an "open house" in a style she has perfected over the years. Once exposed to her charm, folks returned again and again.

The bulk of the books for sale are located on the ground floor. After browsing there for a while, you climb the stairs to the gardening section, then on up to the top floor, which contains the children's books. This is also where the readings are held. At one event, as many as twelve authors all read from their books. We were entertained for four hours!

Thora used one end of the room to set-up the refreshments, which included wine, coffee, a punch bowl filled with either herbal tea or fruit punch, and a lovely assortment of open-faced sandwiches, fresh fruit and cheese, and cakes and deserts. There was very seldom any admission charged. This always puzzled me, until I learned that, in the case of a book launch; the publishers of that particular book almost always help toward the expenses involved.

Many authors who were on a promotional tour, would swing by Nanaimo eventually, and we had the privilege of hearing them at the Bookstore on Bastion Street. Thora always treated new fledgling writers exactly the same as prolific and well-known authors.

When my first book, *Crazy Cooks and Gold Miners* was published, Gordon and I were away on holidays in California, so I never had a real launch, plus I had never even attended one. Apart from a couple of radio interviews and one newspaper review, I escaped much of the publicity (secretly relieved!).

This time, though, it was different. Thora said, "We're going to make this one that nobody will forget." And she went about making posters, sending out invitations and putting announcements in the local newspapers.

"May I help with something?" I offered. But she insisted everything was taken care of. All she needed was a list of my personal friends and acquaintances for the invitations.

The following week was one of extreme ups and downs for me. Half the time I was too thrilled and excited to sleep when bedtime came around, and every other day I would have an attack of nerves. Most of the invitations on my list were really just announcements, because the bulk of my friends and relations were too far away to attend. I even resorted to talking to myself.

"What if nobody comes? What if they aren't interested in the subject matter, and start leaving as I am reading to them? What if they want to ask questions about dates (my bug-a-boo from childhood school days) and my mind goes blank and turns to mush? What if... STOP! If this keeps up, you idiot, you'll be haggard and too exhausted to read with any expression. Okay, but I STILL can't get to sleep!"

Finally, the big day arrived, and our house began filling up. First, our beloved granddaughter Tanja, and her partner, Brent, arrived with a huge bouquet of flowers and fresh oysters for the barbeque we had planned after the launch. Next came our son and his wife. Kirk had just returned home from Venezuela, after being away for three months, and today was his birthday. Our friend, Joan, was with them and they had brought a large cake with "Congratulations Joyce, and Happy Birthday Kirk." All of them had driven a fair distance to get here.

"I'm so glad you made it," I told them. "You may be the only ones there." But after all their good cheer, and a couple of glasses of wine, I was on top of the world and ready for anything.

We all went together, and when we arrived at the bookstore, Kirk helped Gordon up the stairs and Thora led him to a big soft armchair.

Now the place began filling up with people, and I was thrilled to see how many of them I knew. And the rest I remembered from all the other "readings" we had gone to. Soon it was time for Thora to introduce me, and to give the guests a short description of *Yukon Riverboat Days*. There was a brief moment, just as she gave me a little squeeze and walked away leaving me there alone looking out on what seemed like a sea of faces, when I felt the urge to run, but just as quickly it disappeared.

The faces came into focus, and I saw them for what they were-smiling, friendly, warm faces. And as I sat down and opened up my book to read to them, such a feeling of encouragement enveloped me that it could only be described as euphoric!

I read and read, enjoying the stories of those pioneers as much as that crowd seemed to. I could have read to them all night; but I decided to leave them something to read for themselves. Another hour passed, receiving many hugs, signing books and drinking wine. This was definitely one of the highlights of my life.

8

Trip to Whitehorse

Early in July, Gordon and I flew to Whitehorse. We had gone back every year since we moved to Vancouver Island, but this time I wanted to revisit its early days, how it used to be when I was a child. I wanted to remember the way it was before the U.S. Army moved in with their big trucks and earth-moving equipment and started building the Yukon portion of the Alaska Highway.

Not having a car this time around was an advantage. I could start out walking from the Regina Hotel, where we were staying, which is very close and easy walking distance from everything that used to be Whitehorse when I was going to school there. Even though my friend's homes weren't there any more, and the old original businesses were either gone or rebuilt beyond recognition, my feet just seemed to walk me to where the old sites used to be. I remembered most of them; then I would close my eyes and envision them exactly as they were in the past.

The city limits had expanded in every direction, to the extent that the old town-site was only a tiny portion of what it was right up to 1941. But my focus this time was on the old days and landmarks. What made it complete was that I met so many people I knew, just by walking. On all the other trips back home over the years, we had driven the car and hardly ever met anyone we knew. I was beginning to think they had all left the country.

One day, I did the tourist thing and went on a tour of the SS *Klondike*, which has been restored and rests on the bank of the river at the south end of town. Everything on the paddlewheeler looked so new and clean. I found myself wishing they had used old frayed gunnysacks instead, for the fake ore that represented the cargo.

I visualized everything I saw as it had been in the past. In the early days those sacks of silver lead were pretty grimy looking after being piled on the riverbank at Stewart City to await the next boat from Dawson that was pushing an empty barge.

Then I found a spot on the edge of the river; sat on a rock with my feet in the water and just daydreamed for a while, watching the deep green water eddying around the rocks; the strong current swept past me on its way to the Bering Sea. I felt rejuvenated by its vast energy.

That river has claimed many lives and has been silent witness to many human dramas over the past hundred years—broken dreams, heartbreak and great sacrifice. But she's seen victories, too, and thrilling adventure and daring heroism.

The rapids are gone now. My good friend, Gladys and I spent many happy hours at the Whitehorse Rapids. We walked on the narrow-gauge railway out of town, past the roundhouse, until we came to the remains of the old wooden tramway, which was built in 1898 so the stampeders could portage their canoes and gear around the rough water, on their way to the Gold Rush in Dawson City. The tramway was our shortcut to the Rapids, when Gladys and I went on our picnics. We would walk along, shouting to be heard over the rushing noise of the water.

Sitting there on the riverbank, amidst the shimmering green leaves of the aspen trees and the vivid blue and pink of the wild flowers that thrived there, I began to think of winter, when the river would freeze over, and what it must have been like for the mail carriers between Dawson and Whitehorse before the road was built and the boats were all pulled off in the fall.

I thought about people like mail carriers Johnny Hoggan and Ed Whitehouse. Ed's mail-run was 120 miles long and the hardest one in existence. They had to use dogteams in the early days until the tractors came along and years later, of course, the small airplanes.

Sometimes in the fall, the ice floes would jam in the river and pile up twenty feet high in places. The dogs had to work their way over and around these ice boulders with no trail at all to follow. On top of that, they had "shell ice" to contend with; which is what happens when extreme temperatures cause the water to drop away from the ice, leaving a brittle, thin, shell-like surface on top. At times water would get trapped between this shell and the solid ice below, and if the sleds broke through there was a real danger of getting soaked to the skin.

Then they would have to stop and build a big fire on the shoreline in order to dry out. More than a few inexperienced men died on those trails. "Slush" was another danger they faced. When a fresh snowfall hid the water lying on the ice below, a teamster could very easily venture into one of these spots.

When the snowstorms were the heaviest, the dog mushers sometimes had to abandon the sleighs for toboggans, and many times they were forced to snowshoe ahead of the dogs, day after day, making a trail for them to follow. An old, experienced dog was a wonderful asset. He could instinctively sense where the old trail lay, even though it was invisible under the fresh snow. The goal they set for themselves was twenty-five miles a day. If they had been delayed by extra heavy sledding, they would have to make a brush camp along the river, where there was plenty of dry wood, and spend a night in the open.

They fed their dogs cornmeal and grease, cooked in a huge kettle over the campfire. And if the teamster was lucky enough to bag a caribou, they all ate very well for awhile. The winter mail-run lasted five months, from November 15 to April 15, and after that folks would have to wait until the ice was gone from the river to get their mail, when the first paddlewheeler of the season made its way to Dawson City.

I had written what I knew of Ed's story, as in my opinion he had led such a fascinating life. Unfortunately he passed away, just a few weeks before my book came out in print. I was devastated when I heard this; when you have written about someone, even though you haven't met them in person, they become a part of your life somehow. I had wanted him to read the stories.

There was a silver lining to this cloud, however, because I met his son on this trip to Whitehorse.

The owner of Mac's Fireweed Store in Whitehorse did a promotional thing for a book signing I had agreed to, so ten days after we arrived in town, I found myself sitting at a table in autographing copies of *Yukon Riverboat Days*. A lot of people brought in books that they had bought there previously, for me to sign, so I got caught up on their family news. Between that, and the folks I met there for the first time, it turned out to be a very enjoyable experience.

At one point I looked up to see a tall man towering over me with an armful of books. He plopped them down on the table and stuck out a big hand, which totally enveloped my own, making it feel very small indeed.

"I'm Ed Whitehouse's son," he boomed in a deep voice. "I got some books here for you to sign. They're for Ed's grandkids. My dad passed away last month." He went on, "I like what you wrote about him."

He flipped open a book to the chapter on Ed and pointed to the poem I had written at the beginning. (I had tried to find one by Robert Service that fit this story, same as I had done with the others, but nothing I saw seemed to belong to the subject, so I wrote my own instead.)

"It's a good poem," he said, in a much softer voice, so I glanced up again and noticed a couple of tears in the big guy's eyes. He gave me a list of the names, and asked me to write "For Ed Whitehouse's grandson," or granddaughter, as the case might be. He said he would be back to pick them up later and left. It was the highlight of my day.

The next day I took another walk along the riverbank, and on my way home I decided to go and take a look at the "Old Log Church." The one I was faithfully taken to every Sunday of my life, it seems, when I was a child. Often reluctantly I have to say, but still, it held a lot of memories for me. Like the time I disgraced myself singing in the choir.

Among the singers, that evening, was a tall dignified English gentleman, one of the "church pillars," who fancied himself to be a fabulous baritone. Not everyone agreed with him, but of course he had no way of knowing that. At the end of every verse, this night, he held the last note long after everyone else had stopped singing. This tickled my funny bone for some reason (probably something to do with being thirteen years old) and I got the giggles...bad news! I tried to choke them back with all my might, but there was no way it could be done and nowhere to turn. I was crowded in between two serious-looking matrons.

The choir started in on another hymn now, and the man really held on to that last note this time. I became hysterical. In the silence that followed, my sobbing was the only sound in that church. Or so I thought.

The minister gave me a grave look from his pulpit and announced in a solemn tone, "Joyce, you may be excused if you'd like some fresh air." They all made room for me to get by, and I ran out into the night. Once outside, I was crying for real now. I walked and walked the quiet streets, all alone and disgraced.

"What will Mother and Dad say?" And the thought brought more tears and a desire to run away and never come back. It seemed like hours later when I finally got up the nerve to face the music. Timidly, I opened the door to our house. My distraught mother was crying, "Where have you been? Don't you know we've been worried sick?"

"Now, Mother," said Dad, "It's all right, she's home safe and sound." He took me in his arms for a big hug.

"I'll never, ever go to church again," I sobbed, "And you can't make me!"

Mom was smiling again now, and she told me, "You needn't feel bad, child, everyone in that church had the giggles. Didn't you notice the organist's shoulders? She was laughing so hard she could hardly play the organ!"

I was astounded. "Giggling? Oh, Mom, you're not serious!"

"On my word of honor," she declared. Relief flooded through me. I felt like thanking God, right there, that I had such wonderful parents, even though I wasn't in church!

My thoughts returned to the present now. I turned the corner and there it stood. Exactly the same as when I was baptized, confirmed and married in it.

The Old Log Church had been converted into a small museum. They had erected walls and panels covered with archival material that really took up most of the space and obliterated any semblance of the old ambiance that pervaded that holy place in the old days.

A young women in her early twenties was filling the visitors in on the early history of the church in a very confident and authoritative manner. I listened in amazement, as I looked at the old pictures. At one point she was telling them a story that was so outrageous that I found it very hard to maintain my silence.

When the group of about six people left, I lingered behind. "Excuse me," I said to the girl, "I hope you don't mind me telling you this, but someone has misinformed you about one of your stories." She shot me an annoyed look, and impatiently waited for me to continue.

"I happened to have been here, during that time period," I told her, "and I know that not to be true. You see, I was born here in Whitehorse, and I came here every Sunday. Please don't take this as criticism, because it's not intended to be. Just thought you'd like to know the true facts."

"Oh, I've heard it all before," she said. "This is how I was instructed to inform the people, and it's not going to change." With that she turned her back and began reading her book again.

I left the old building with a sense of loss and sadness in the knowledge that history was being corrupted here, and I wasn't too sure that anyone cared. It was a lonesome feeling.

About 500 feet from the old church was the new (comparatively speaking) Christ Church Cathedral. I had heard about the wonderful stained glass windows, designed by our own Yukon artist Ted Harrison, so thought I would just skip over there and have a look.

Immersed in my own thoughts, I noticed vaguely that the sidewalk between the two buildings was cordoned off with yellow tape, and I could see three or four workmen way up ahead doing something around the cathedral. A new plaque caught my eye that I hadn't seen before. It was across the sidewalk, so I ducked under the tape (no one was working right there) and stood on the walk reading the inscription. All of a sudden I felt a very strange sensation. Thoughts of an impending earthquake crossed my mind, but no, it wasn't that, just a weird sinking sensation.

A loud shout startled me out of my wits: "Oh man, no! Jesus Lady, get the f—— off, damn it!"

Only then did it strike me—I was sinking into freshly poured cement! In the blink of an eye I leaped off the new sidewalk, mortified to say the least.

When I had composed myself, I thought, "Well! I'm not going to let those guys intimidate me!" Boldly I kept right on walking in their direction, my head up bravely. Not daring to look at them, however, I sang out "Sorry!" as I went by with a sheepish grin on my face. This cracked them up and they all burst out laughing.

Once out of sight, I scraped the cement off my shoes. Somehow I felt young, light-hearted and carefree as I entered the new cathedral. I spent some time admiring the new stained glass windows. What a nice tribute to Ted, I thought.

The next day I casually sauntered by the same location. The yellow tape was gone, but where I had hoped to find my foot-prints, enshrined forever in the sidewalk; all that was visible was a couple of dirty-looking rough marks, where they had evidently tried to repair the damage. Oh, well, so much for my dreams of posterity!

I won't go into details about the Regina Hotel where we stayed, having talked about it before in my "Yukon Childhood" chapter, except to say that my school chum Goody and her brother John were still running it. They had leased out the restaurant part to Louis Irvine's daughter and his three granddaughters. I remember Louis quite clearly. He had died about a year previous. When we met his family at the hotel, I was overwhelmed at the welcome we received. It turned out they had all bought *Yukon Riverboat Days* because of the short story I had written about their beloved Louis. They were all very friendly and nice people, and the service we received was the very best. In fact, between Louis' family and the hotel proprietors we were spoiled rotten.

We spent a couple of days with our dear friends, Tom and Tammy, and Paul Banks, where the hospitality, as always, was so warm and homey that we hated to leave.

After that, we enjoyed a week with my daughter Norma and Cal. Norma had taken some time off from her work, and we had a really good visit. Finally it was time to drive to the airport, and our trip down memory lane was over, for this year anyway. It had been a good one.

9

Letters to Friends

July 15, 1992

Hi Mabel and Jim,

I'm writing this "on the road." We're on our way home to Vancouver Island, from Whitehorse, and right now we're heading for Prince George. It is still 300 miles away, though, as we've just come over the Cassiar-Stewart Road. The highways were all in good shape, except for the construction areas, which were dusty and rough. We came through one of these when it was raining. We're towing my car behind the camper, so you can imagine how our outfit looks now! We'll stop in Hazelton and find a carwash. Should be at Herb and Millie's tomorrow. I'm sure looking forward to seeing them and having a soak in their hot tub!

I flew up north to Whitehorse on June 3. Gordon and Kirk had gone up in April with the pickup, and Gordon towed my Volkswagen up then.

While we were there, Gordon and I took the three-and-a-half-hour return trip from Skagway on the old White Pass and Yukon Route narrow-gauge railway—a gift from my daughter Norma and her husband Cal. The train used to run from Skagway to Whitehorse, 110 miles, but when it became no longer an asset financially, the White Pass terminated the operation. It was started again as a tourist attraction, to the summit only (about forty miles roundtrip). They stop at points of interest to let you take pictures. It was a spectacular and nostalgic trip for us, as we had met each other for the first time on that train in the fall of 1941.

In 1942 Gordon took on a contract with the White Pass to supply telephone poles from Skagway to Whitehorse along that same route. And a couple of years after that he was supplying the Railroad ties for the White Pass from his sawmill in the Carcross area. We could still see some of the old pole line in places.

Last winter we found a darling little Chihuahua terrier in Palm Springs to replace Freddy, the one we lost last year. This one should have been Freddy #4, but she happened to be a female. Her name is Shelby, but she agreeably answers to Freddy as well, because we keep forgetting and call her that out of habit. She's black, with white feet and chest, a year and a half old and personality-wise she's just like Fred. So Gordon has a "buddy" again. He took her up north with him in April.

I couldn't be happier with my new computer. It's a beauty...such a luxury to have all that memory, speed and color. Had a hard time dragging myself away from it to go north in June.

Our fiftieth anniversary is on the twenty-fourth of this month. We all decided to celebrate it in the fall, maybe September, as it is a better time for the whole family to get together. We'll make it a family reunion at the same time.

How goes the battle for you two? Hope you are both well and happy. We did so enjoy your company last winter in the desert. Think of you often, and hope sometime we'll all get together again. I'm afraid that with Kirk away, and our mine in Dawson "on hold," Gordon's going to find time heavy on his hands again. Nice if he and Jim could get together and do some more "over the table" mining again!

If the Venezuela thing turns out as hoped, Kirk may just sell Gold Bottom. This spring they stripped the high bank on the left side of the creek, right down to the permafrost and found some old-timers' tunnels and shafts forty feet or so below the surface (just above the present creek bed level). It looks very interesting, but it was still too frozen to work when we left there, although melting rapidly every day now that it's exposed. Big chunks of mud, rock and trees are falling down into the creek, even as you watch. Lots of prehistoric bones, etc., in that area.

The old-timers never had the equipment to work that kind of ground extensively, had to thaw it out with little fires to sink their shafts, so it is virtually still virgin ground. If the South

American venture doesn't work out, Kirk will monitor the bank down with water pressure, build new settling ponds and put the material through the trammel. He says he will sell the ground now though if someone's interested. It should be a good deal for somebody, as he is including enough equipment to mine it, for example, the D-9 Cat, loader and trammel, pumps and lots of parts and small equipment plus the camp trailers (equipped).

The assessment work is all done and registered for several years in advance. If you hear of anyone interested, get him or her to contact us for details. The property is comprised of fifteen claims, all in good standing. Gold Bottom was one of the main Gold Rush areas in the early days; the first place they spotted gold. It became a community of over 10,000 population. Very few signs of it are left now. One advantage to our property is that the big gold dredges never did work that part of the ground when they operated.

Well, guys, hope this finds you both "in the pink," and who knows...maybe we'll run into each other again on the desert next winter!

All the best,

September, 1992

Dear Dixie and Lloyd,

We're back home on the Island. Kirk's wife Gunn, and our daughter, Norma (who flew over from Whitehorse with husband, Cal, and daughter, Kris), hosted a fiftieth anniversary party for us in Gunn's home in Duncan. Actually, our anniversary was July 24, but it wasn't convenient to have a get-together then. It was like a family reunion. Just about everyone was there, except Kirk and Ted, who were unfortunately too far away. Gordon's three sisters and his brother came over from the mainland, as well as my sister and brother, so the whole thing was a huge success. The care and preparation they put into the event was just phenomenal. They gave us celebration we'll never forget, and that night when we got home I couldn't sleep because my heart was so full...just

125

kept thinking about how lucky we are...belonging to this family and having such good friends as well. And I thought about the ones who couldn't be there, too.

Kirk will be home, with Gunn and their two daughters, Naomi and Tanja, for Christmas.

Our grandson, Kurt, (Norma and Cal's son) and Lisa had a brand new baby girl Brittni, in October. We haven't seen her yet, but she is our first great-grandchild, so we're very excited about this. And Gordon thought he was pretty smart, sleeping with a *grandmother*. Hey, he hadn't even lived yet! Another milestone this year is getting my book *Crazy Cooks and Gold Miners* published. It has been a very rewarding and enjoyable experience, apart from the suspense of waiting to actually see it in print. So we'll be seeing it on the book shelves before spring.

We wish you the very best for the New Year, and hope you have the nicest Christmas ever!

Love,

In August of 1993, we flew back up to Whitehorse for the Lambert Street School reunion, where we met a lot of people I grew up with, some I hadn't seen for more than fifty years. Among these were actually three of my former schoolteachers. One lady, Estelle Cameron, had taught me in grades two and three. The party went on for four days at various locations, and we had a fabulous time. Then it was back to the Island again.

Shortly after this, there was a rather abrupt change of plans in our lives. Norma, our daughter, who is in real estate, had called us from Whitehorse, just to let us know that the gentleman who had bought our house in Carcross in 1960, was planning to sell. When Gordon heard this, he couldn't get it out of his mind. I love the Island, but Gordon never quite got used to it and never felt really at home there. Nothing I could say would dissuade him from selling out in Saltaire and returning to the Yukon to live, even though it was the last thing in the world I wanted to do at our age.

He had forgotten the implications of trying to fit our furniture into the small home he had built there in the 1940s. "We'll manage," he kept on saying. Seeing that he was really set on this, I went along with the idea, thinking that just maybe we could build an extension onto it. But I suspected he was in the first stages of Alzheimer's, and I agreed with a heavy heart. His sister, Phyllis, couldn't get over the idea that we were going back to Carcross. I wrote these poems on one of my sad days.

On Returning to the Yukon

She looks at me and just shakes her head,
With that half-angry expression I've started to dread.
"You're going back THERE?" she said,
"It's quite beyond me, why a person would go-
Back there to the land of the cold and the snow.
Any reason at all I can't figure out.
That you're sane, normal people I'm beginning to doubt."
"Well, what would you do?" I answered at last.
"He wants to go back to the home of his past.
If we stay he's unhappy...we go I feel sad.
I can cope with this problem, now is that so bad?
Should I make him stay here, to be lonely and blue?
Well, you are his sister...just what would you do?"

The Seeds of Bitterness

"It's so wonderful," they cry,
"You're going back, how exciting!"
"Your life has gone full circle!"
"It was meant to be...it's where you belong."
"How romantic, you must write a sequel to your book!"
Before the circle closes, I guess they mean. Ironic.
But happiness can never be found at the expense of another.
It is non-interchangeable.
Maybe someday I'll look on this day in a different light.
And these seeds of bitterness will sprout
In a new happier form, and the tears in my heart will become flowers.

Goodbye

Goodbye Chemainus
I'll cry for you.
All your hopes and expectations—your disappointments.
The goals that you set...many reached, some unattained.
The friendly faces, and the bitter ones.
"Look at our town," some say, "Our wonderful cheerful town.
Years ago it was sad...run down, disillusioned and dying."
Others complain, "It's not enough, the planners promised us more.
They failed—look at the money it has cost us.
These people are dreamers, not businessmen."
Maybe. But this is what I see when I experience Chemainus.
Delight in the faces of the visitors...
Delight and pleasure and amazement and fun.
I see pride and friendliness in the eyes of the store owners,
And a cornucopia of beautiful handcrafted treasures in the shops.
I see history depicted in breathtaking murals,
Created with love and talent on the walls of the town.

Goodbye Saltair
Driving through the lush green paradise of the countryside,
I pray that at least this little part of your world remains
Untouched and unchanged by human hands.
Daily though, the insidious creeping signs of commercialism
Are gaining momentum;
Ripping up your roots, and replacing them with concrete.
I recognize the feeling.
My life, too, is being uprooted,
And my heart, right now, feels like concrete inside me.

Goodbye Vancouver
I'll miss your majestic sky-line,
Driving across Lions Gate Bridge;
Looking down on boats cutting across the water.
Seeing Stanley Park and the marinas below.
Ahead...the magical elegance of the White Sails;
A reminder of the glorious Expo days.
I'll miss the hustle and bustle of Granville St.
The adventure of exploring new areas of this cosmopolitan city,
And the relief of going back home to the "Island,"
After the thrill wears off once more, and the feet begin to hurt.
I'll come back some day.

128

May 1993

Dear Dixie and Lloyd,

Well, here we are in Whitehorse. Gordon's brother Bill kindly offered to help him move. They got here ten days ahead of me, Gordon driving the pickup and camper and Bill the Mercedes. They took enough household stuff with them to last us three months, including my big computer and printer, which took up the whole trunk of the car by themselves. If the house in Ladysmith sells right away, of course, we'll have to fly back to the island and ship all the stuff to Carcross that I have packed down the basement.

They left me to pack everything except the furniture in nine days, as my ticket was booked for that time. I must have 100 boxes ready down the basement (fifteen of them are books alone!). There is not a thing left upstairs, all the cupboards empty, even the pictures off the walls. What a job.

The day before I was to leave for Vancouver, I knew I just couldn't make it without help, so, being exhausted, I sent a plea to Tanja and Brent in Port Alberni to come and help with the last odds and ends. They came to my rescue and helped for a few hours, thank goodness. The next day I left by bus with five huge suitcases, all by myself. What a hassle. That is a story in itself, but too long to tell here. The short of it is that I took the car as far as Kirk and Gunn's house in Duncan, where I was going to leave it until we came back to the Island.

They were both away, so I parked it and took a taxi to the bus depot, where I booked a ride to Vancouver, juggling the suitcases all the way. When I got to the Vancouver bus depot, I rushed to load the suitcases on the shuttle bus to the airport to catch the plane in time. I had to end up sending a couple of the largest suitcases ahead by Greyhound to Whitehorse, as it was too much for me to handle alone.

I arrived here, to find Gordon and Shelby at the airport to meet me. Billy had gone back to Langley by then. They didn't seem to have any plans, the camper was out at Norma and Cal's, thirty miles out of town, and I didn't really feel all that much like driving out there just then.

Norma had made arrangements for us to rent a small cabin in Carcross after June 10, where we were to stay until our own house there became available in September. I had hoped that Gordon would have found a rooming house or something to stay in besides the camper until then, but no, I guess he was waiting for me to arrive first. By this time all the tension, packing, etc., had caught up with me, I guess, and I was in no mood to do anything except go to bed and rest. So I made him book in at a new motel that had recently been built there in Whitehorse. I woke up the next morning with a fever and sore throat, aching from head to foot, and with a huge cold-sore to boot. For that whole week I so sick I hardly got out of bed at all. At least they let us keep Shelby in the room. She loved it.

Anyway, I slowly recovered, and we went out to see Norma and Cal. The following weekend we drove over to Carcross. It was absolutely beautiful there (this has been the nicest spring I can ever remember up here), and I was beginning to feel that we had made the right choice after all.

I love the Island, but Gordon never quite got used to it and never felt really at home. Now that we were here, though, I felt that we should give the Yukon another try, for a year anyway, and see how we both feel then. I've always missed the early spring here, the sky so blue against the white sparkly snow.

I called the man who was still occupying the house, to ask if I might just drop around to have a look at it, to give me a better idea of how much of our furniture would fit into the rooms.

What a surprise when I did call him. So that, of course, was the end of that. I politely told him that apparently the whole thing had been a misunderstanding, and we would certainly make other arrangements for living quarters. We have now totally given up on the idea.

Now Gordon has decided that maybe we'd be better off going back to the Island and finding another place there instead of building in Carcross. On top of that he is now in a hurry to get going. But one thing is for sure. He had better not change his mind again this time, because I'm not going to go through all this a second time.

Our house in Saltair has apparently sold; the buyers have put a substantial down payment on it and it has to be vacated before Aug.3. So I guess we really should start for home again by next week, if we have to find a place and get moved in by then. Not looking forward to the long drive back in the camper (but I'm so secretly glad to be going back to the Island). I guess we'll ship the car (that Billy drove up here for us) loaded with my computer, etc., down to Vancouver by White Pass container and pick it up when we get there.

One happy note, though, Mac's Fireweed book store has sold their first shipment of *Crazy Cooks* already and their second one is due any day. I've had to autograph a whole raft of them for people, and they seem to be really enjoying the book. The Yukon Gallery is getting in a batch, as well as Maxmillian's store in Dawson, and they all want to have a "signing" later on during the tourist season. Guess we won't be here then, but it was the thought that counted.

Before leaving for home, Gordon and I took a drive to Skagway. The scenery was superb. Tutshi Lake was like a mirror, the rivers are all high now and racing like rapids, and all the waterfalls spilling down over the steep banks along the road. Skagway itself was so lush and green, and warm, just a fresh light breeze to keep it from being too hot, and the wonderful clean air. I could easily become hooked on this country again, now that we're away from muddy old mining camps, but I guess it just wasn't meant to be. Torn two ways, aren't I? I won't complain about the beautiful coast of B.C. either when we get back.

Love,

July 18, 1993 (back in Ladysmith in our same house...)

Dear Dixie and Lloyd,

As you can see, I have been so unsettled that I never even got your letter mailed. Well, things don't stay constant very long in this family! I can't believe the changes that have occurred so rapidly this summer. We have found a place. Decided to try condo living now. No upkeep, no stairs, easy living befitting people our age. Guess a person has to learn when to let go and quit fighting the odds. I think you're going to like our new apartment, and just remember it will always be your "home away from home" too, when you come to visit us. We're buying a beautiful brand new suite in a complex on the ocean, at a fraction of the cost a regular home would be in the same type of environment. It's located on a kind of peninsula that juts out into the water right where the Gabriola ferry lands, behind Harbour Park Mall in Nanaimo on Cameron Island. There is a marina on one side of us and the open ocean right at our doorstep on the other side. Gordon has actually shown some enthusiasm for this move; so I guess things all work out for the best in the long run. I feel so thankful. It has always been my dream to live close to the water again. Don't know what I've done to deserve it. We can hardly wait to get into it. We are on the ground floor, and there's a spare bedroom and bathroom (just waiting for you.)

We hear by the grapevine that you're planning a trip in August, so really looking forward to seeing you.

Love you both,

Christmas Letter, 1998

Dear Folks,

Just to bring you up on some of the latest happenings around here.

The doorbell rang at 10:00 a.m. sharp, just as I was cramming the last item into my suitcase. It was the taxi driver, arriving to take us to the bus station, where we'd be leaving for Victoria, two hours south. From there we would catch the airport shuttle to our plane and fly to Kelowna, where Gordon's brother Bill would meet us and drive us to Sicamous, a forty-five-minute drive.

Our hotel there was already booked for the next three days. All this was in preparation for a trip to the interior of B.C. for the wedding of our granddaughter Naomi to Derek.

Since the alarm clock had gone off at 8:00, just two hours earlier, I had checked my e-mail, showered, made two beds and fixed breakfast (grapefruit, scrambled eggs sausages, toast, spiced

132

peach jam, and coffee), loaded the dishwasher, wiped kitchen counters, put on my face, finger combed my hair, helped Gordon dress and shave, watered the plants and unplugged the electric appliances.

So why didn't I set the alarm for seven instead of eight and save myself the mad rush? Good question. Maybe, subconsciously, I like the challenge of living on the edge—the satisfaction of thinking, "Wow! I've done it again. Got there on time!" Or maybe I just can't resist that extra hour of sleep. I don't know, but I HATE it when I do that...

Bad enough that I tossed and turned most of the night, and when I finally fell into a fitful sleep, I had this crazy dream about being lost in a vast jungle of very tall grass. I kept pushing it aside, trying to see where I was. Suddenly something bumped into me and I screamed. What a relief to see it was only Michael Douglas with his big lion gun pointing at me.

"God," he said, "I could have shot you. I thought you were a lion! Don't you be frightened, I'll keep you safe..."

I felt warm and fuzzy and protected. Just my luck though, I woke up right about then...but I digress. Back to our trip.

The taxi driver unloaded our luggage on the tarmac, beside the bus marked Victoria and Gordon waited outside on a bench while I dashed into the office to get our tickets.

The passengers were already boarding. We watched an elderly man being helped on while the driver loaded his electric scooter into a luggage department under the bus. Gordon has one of those, like a plush battery-driven armchair on wheels, and I was glad to realize that option would be available to us also, if we needed it.

This was a sight-seeing tour bus, and we sat high in the front seat, which allowed a panoramic view of the countryside. Traveling over the Malahat Summit was a gorgeous trip. The yellow broom was out in profusion, its blazing color providing an almost startling contrast to the evergreens. Hillsides covered with purple lupins and the fresh green leaves of the aspen trembling in the breeze. Western British Columbia gets a fair amount of rain (well, sometimes lots of rain) in the winter months, but the lush growth in the spring makes it all worthwhile. I've seen ninety days in a row of sunshine and blue skies one summer.

As we got closer to Victoria, the bus began stopping at all the stops to pick up passengers, and I began worrying if we'd get there on time. It was already past the time I'd asked the shuttle bus to pick us up. When we arrived at the depot and I rushed in to phone them again.

"Oh," the girl in the office told me, "They were just there ten minutes ago, and there was nobody waiting so they left."

Hurriedly, I told her we would miss our plane if we waited for the next one, and while I stayed on hold, she actually found the driver on his pager. He turned around and came back for us. We were the only passengers aboard. I guess it was because everyone else had the sense to get there on time. I hadn't allowed for the stops the main bus had to make en-route, between Nanaimo and Victoria.

It was a forty-five-minute drive to the airport, and we hit every red light along the route. By the time we got there I was resigned to having a four-hour wait until the next plane.

"It left ten minutes ago," I told Gordon.

Wonder of wonders, when the terminal came into view, there it was still on the runway. I don't know if they had waited on us, or if there had been some other delay, but I was so glad when an attendant hurried over with a wheelchair for Gordon. We boarded the plane just before it lifted off, and I sunk back in my seat with a huge sigh of relief, as the tension at last began to drain away. I'll never cut it that close again, I told myself for the hundredth time.

From then on, everything fell into place like clockwork. Billy was there to pick us up in Kelowna with his van, and an hour later we were pulling into the hotel in Sicamous. One day to rest and look around town, visit the family, and then it was time to help decorate a hall, arrange what seemed like a truckload of flowers, set up tables and centerpieces, make boutonniere and bouquets and corsages. Streamers and balloons galore. Kirk and Gunn were planning on having the flower arrangements done by a florist in town, but luckily their close friends, Barb and Lowry, were there. They had owned flower and balloon stores in Whitehorse, until they retired in Arizona a year ago. They wouldn't hear of anyone else doing it but them, and they are true professionals when it comes to flowers and decorating. We were all so thankful for their wonderful contribution of time and expertise.

Kirk and Gunn are the sort of people who never lose touch with any of the friends they have made over the years—and they came from all over. A lot of them had come to the Yukon in the sixties and are now living in B.C. They were there with their own families, so it was a great reunion as well.

The wedding in the church was lovely, as are all weddings. This one was unique in that Naomi and Derek's little one-year-old daughter, Madison, attended. Naomi and her dad, walked up the aisle towards the groom and bridesmaids, and right behind them the baby was being pulled along in a little red wagon, smiling and waving her hands and looking so adorable in her tiny white lacy dress. She was deposited in the lap of Derek's mother, in the front row, where she proceeded to watch and listen to the ceremony with great interest. The minister included her, by name, in his preliminary to the ceremony. When the time came to sign the register, Naomi held out her arms for the baby, signed her own name, and then guided the pen in Madison's fingers so she signed too. Then it was Derek's turn. It added so much to all the things that go with weddings. It was truly a nineties wedding. My grandparents would have rolled over in their graves.

The wedding party departed for the picture taking ordeal, and an hour or two later it was time for the reception and catered dinner in the hall. Tanja and a friend were lovely in short, satin, red fitted dresses with red high-heeled sandals, and the men looked smashing alongside them in their black tuxedos and red boutonnieres. Naomi was radiant and glowing in her flowing white satin gown and veil. Derek made the most touching and loving speech I have ever heard, declaring his love for her and Madison all over again, which made Naomi cry, along with half the women in the hall. I was so proud of him and my whole family.

Tanja's fiancé, Richard, was the master of ceremonies and DJ, and did a super job at the mike. There was a no-host bar, and by the time dinner was over the noise level was unbelievable—250 people and much music and hilarity. The acoustics left much to be desired, it was held upstairs in the legion and the ceiling was not very high. When it got too noisy for us old folks, Billy

135

drove Gordon and I back to our hotel, and that was enough for one day!

The bride and groom received a great gift—the use of a deluxe houseboat for two days, from a friend of theirs. Sicamous is located on a beautiful lake, which is about 100 miles long. It is the houseboat capitol of Canada, apparently, and most of them were there in the marina, or on the lake, right in view of our hotel. They spent the night there and planned on taking it out on the lake a couple of days later.

The following day, we caught a ride home with Tanja and Richard in their van. We drove to Vancouver, took the ferry to Nanaimo; they dropped us off and went on to their home in Courtenay, another hour's drive. Altogether a very fulfilling trip, and we fell into bed tired, but happy.

Hope you have a wonderful Christmas and that 1999 will be a good year.

10

Trying Times

Not long after we moved into the condo, Gordon began having a series of mini-strokes. I never knew when I would wake up at night and find him in a heap on the floor, unable to get up by himself. Several times I had to call a neighbor to help me get him back in bed; twice it was necessary to call an ambulance to take him to emergency in the hospital. The doctors suggested I should start looking into finding a care home for him.

Everyone who has had to go through that procedure knows it has to be the hardest thing one does in a lifetime. It was a heart-wrenching family decision, which was taken against his wishes.

Silently Slipping Away

Hour after hour he lies there;
oblivious of life going on around him,
sometimes sleeping, sometimes just staring at the ceiling
or at the TV without really seeing it;
aimlessly flicking from channel to channel.
Not caring that just outside the window,
there are sailboats on the water
and the harbor is alive with boats of all shapes and sizes.
People are walking together, in pairs or in groups,
watching the activity.
He gets up for meals, painfully and slowly;
after being called a dozen times.
Sometimes I say, "I'll bring it to you,"
but he doesn't want that.

After the meal he goes back to the couch again.
"Talk to me like you used to," I plead silently,
knowing that he doesn't want to hear it.
It's so lonesome—never getting an answer, or an opinion,
or any feedback to my attempts at conversation.
But now I no longer expect any communication.
Friends seldom come to visit anymore;
he won't talk to them either, and not understanding,
I think they go away hurt,
even though I've tried to fill the gap with chatter.
It's depression from the stroke, the doctors say,
and he's never adjusted to retirement...lost interest in life.
I throw myself into my work, to preserve my sanity.
Spend hours at my computer,
trying to block out the knowledge that he's sad and lonely;
nothing I can say or do helps, no matter how I try.
Sometimes I feel a great anger, at the injustice of it all.
Once in awhile I go out walking by myself,
I should spend more time with friends—I know;
but he hates an empty house, and when I get home
the silent reproach in his face fills me with guilt.
It's getting harder to sleep at night.
If I could have one wish it would be for him to be happy.
It's a selfish one, I know, for the happiness would be mine too...
instead of this lonely existence, and the fear
that after all these years together,
he's silently slipping away from me.

For the next few months most of my time was spent at the care home with him. Traveller's Lodge, it is called, a very friendly, well-run facility with excellent meals and scheduled entertainment for the guests. The nurses there went out of their way to care for the well-being of the tenants. It was not an easy job, but they really tried.

I started having my dinner there every night. On weekends I would bring him home; but this didn't work out, because it was such a trauma to get him into the car when it was time to go back. My son, eventually, had to drive all the way from Chemainus to help me persuade him. So we had to give that up. His room at the lodge was very comfortable. We bought a television with a large screen, which he wouldn't watch, a tape player for music, family pictures, but he had no interest in anything. I had decided eventually, in my mind, to bring him home again, but my son and the doctor would not hear of it. He kept getting out of bed in the Lodge and falling. Each time it would take two nurses to get him back up. My husband was six feet one and weighted 200 pounds. I turned to poetry.

Today I'll be Happy

Today I'll be happy,
I'll be cheerful and bright,
Speak about the good times,
And old friends; the ones still with us.
Speaking of old friends—where are they lately?
They don't come around much any more (the ones still with us)
Maybe they, too, are withdrawing
Into their lonely cocoons...
Waiting for a metamorphosis to set them free.
But I must not think these things.
At intervals I stop talking,
Give you a chance...just in case.
I'll keep my comments light and uplifting.
One-sided conversation, never ending.
I try, "Remember when?"
But you stare straight ahead,
And my words fall on empty ears.
And my good intentions
Come crashing down.

Sitting in the Silence

Silently they sit; eyes averted
Looking down at nothing,
Or staring at a spot on the wall.
I sit beside my husband;
Glance around the dining room.

He is one of them now.
His silence, like theirs,
Broken only by the rattling of the dishes in the kitchen
And the forced cheerfulness of the staff's voices
As they pass around the food.
What are they thinking, these old ones?
Each absorbed in a world of their own,
Oblivious to every other being in the room.
Impossible to tell whether they are content with their memories;
Or just waiting for an "angel" to come and rescue them.
Some you can tell are anxious, feeling trapped and abandoned.
One walks continuously around and around in circles,
*   like a caged animal.*
Another calls out a name, repeatedly,
"Sue, come and get me, please, Sue, come and get me."
A little white-haired lady across the room
Rocks back and forth,
Chanting endlessly, "amen, amen…"
Dinner over, they file out of the dining room,
Pushing their walkers or wheelchairs.
I look at my husband, as I help him into his wheel-chair
And I recognize the question in his eyes.
"When are you going to take me home?"
If I only could, my darling,
If we could simply turn back the clock,
I'd take you home in a heartbeat.

We had suspected it for a long time, before booking Gordon into the lodge; but now the doctor had confirmed that he definitely had vascular dementia.

I was eventually able to accept the fact that help is available for caregivers, too. I was dangerously near a nervous breakdown before I did something about it. When professional therapy didn't help Gordon, I knew it was up to me to look after him. And in order to do that, I had to have help myself, in the form of counseling, an anti-depressant and a support group.

I hope I haven't made anyone sad by talking about this. The only reason I decided to reveal this chapter of our lives is in the hope that if there's anyone out there who has a spouse or parent in the same situation, please, please, don't try to cope by your-self. There's help to be had, and you are able to help your dear ones much better by not getting rundown. It took me a long time to realize this. I kept hoping he would get better, even though he hadn't talked to anyone for over a year.

When

"When did you start?" they asked me.
And suddenly I knew.
I started writing when...you stopped talking.
I had no one else to turn to,
Except me.
I had relied on you for too long.
So my thoughts, instead of going into your ears,
Ended up on a piece of white paper,
Instead.
Because you couldn't hear me.
Maybe if I show you in written word,
Remind you in this way, of the good times.
You may read the words, and see
That they are not lost, my darling,
As long as we remember.
And if memories are all we have now,
We'll enjoy them even more.
If we can share them together.
Don't shut me out of your life,
Because I still need you.

Dreams

The medication I was on at this time had a side effect that was quite unexpected. I began having the most unusual and enter-taining dreams. And the best part of all was that I remembered them the next morning. I would wake up and quickly write them down while they were still in memory. Here are a few that I kept.

Fish Dream

In my dream I was taking a solitary walk along the pebble beach, just before the last rays of the sun disappeared below the horizon.

I noticed a beautiful little orange-colored tropical fish about six inches long, flopping along behind me making a futile effort to keep up. A weak, insistent little peep was coming from it. It didn't seem at all strange that a fish would be peeping, but nothing in a dream usually makes sense anyway. I realized the little thing wanted me to pick it up. One of its fins had been injured so it couldn't swim.

A great compassion enveloped me, and I stooped to pick up the fish. Carrying it tenderly in my hands, I walked along the beach toward the place where I had left my friends sitting around their campfires.

Suddenly the little fish wriggled out of my grasp and fell into the water. It'll drown I thought, panic-stricken. The next thing I remember I was swimming around underwater in the darkness, frantically searching for my fish, which somehow was now my child, running my hands over the pebbles on the bottom of the ocean, praying and pleading with God to help me find my baby. It seemed that I searched like this for miles, before giving up and coming to the surface, empty-handed and exhausted.

In my grief, I started over to the closest shadowy figure I could see, sitting by his campfire. In the dim light from the flames he looked at me with accusing eyes and turned away. I ran over to the next campfire, then the next. One by one they looked at me with hooded eyes and turned their backs. I walked away, alone and heartbroken, feeling a pain so intense that it woke me up.

My pillow was wet with tears, and the sense of bereavement so strong that I couldn't immediately shake it off. Not wanting to go back to sleep for a long time, I got up, made some hot chocolate and returned to bed with a book to read.

Wax Museum

In this dream I was searching for Gordon in an old Wild West-type prairie town. There appeared to be no one living in the town. If so, they were all out of sight. A few country stores seemed to be open, the shelves stocked, as if the owners had just stepped out for a minute. Wandering down a worn wooden sidewalk, I finally came to a saloon-type building that had loud, jazzy music coming from it. As I stepped through the door the music stopped, and I went into a dimly lit corridor with a row of benches along each wall. On these benches sat two rows of men and women facing each other, smoking and drinking beer; most of them wore cowboy hats and western boots. The strange thing about them was that they were motionless—all seemed to be frozen in animated gestures, some of them with a bottle raised halfway to their lips or stubbing a cigarette out in an ashtray.

"Oh!" I thought, "It's a wax museum—how lifelike! How in the world can they make the smoke so real?" (It was actually curling up from the ashtrays; the air itself was smoky.)

"Now that's being too realistic," I thought irritably; it was making me cough.

"I'm getting out of here."

As I turned to leave, I noticed the black-bearded fellow on the end of the bench was moving his eyes to follow me.

"Why this whole thing is a hoax!" I thought. Indignantly I turned to face them all.

"I'm on to you," I told them. "You can quit this game whenever you like. And tell me what you did with my husband!"

With this they stood up and began rallying around me. As the music started up again, a feeling of claustrophobia nearly overcame me. I managed to get through the crowd and back out again on the street. The town people had come out of hiding. A man with a familiar, kind and friendly face came up to me and said, "What in the world are you doing here?" I told him I was looking for Gordon, and he said, "Well, just wait here until I get a drink and I'll help you."

He went to a wicket on the outside wall of the building, where a girl stood behind a window with a small opening in it, apparently for cash transactions like at a movie theatre. Inside the booth was a crude, complicated mechanism that dispensed liquor into a glass, then dropped it down an old iron spiral pipe with the end projected out onto a ledge where one picked up their drink.

While I waited for him, another man came staggering up to the booth. He tripped and fell at my feet and, unable to get up again, clutched at one of my ankles and held on for dear life. I tried in vain to shake him off, but he just hung on. When I looked around for help from my friend, he had disappeared. I had to hobble down the street with the fellow still clinging to my ankle.

At last I shook him off and went into what seemed to be a

restaurant, with big round tables that were loaded with delicious-looking food. I sat down at one of them, just as a waitress came along. She gathered up all the clean silverware and carried it off somewhere. Suddenly, out of the blue, Gordon appeared and said, "Did you order?"

"No," I told him, "The food was already here, but we can't eat it because there aren't any knives and forks, and it looks like the waitress has gone home."

"Well, you might just as well wake up then," he said.

Earthquake Dream

I was with a little group of women who seemed to be living in a dry, sandy cavern, which had been gauged out of a barren hill that towered above us. I don't remember any houses being there. My daughter-in-law, Gunn, came over to me all excited, and said, "You have to join us; all the women have decided to pick a date to climb the hill and hurl ourselves over the edge!"

"Why?" I asked.

"It'll be great," she said, "You'll see. We'll all go together."

"You'll be killed!" I shouted.

She laughed merrily and said, "That's okay..."

"No! It's NOT!"

"You're coming, too, Mom," she said.

Visions of us all plunging to our death came to me. I told her, "You're insane! No way will I do that, and I'm not going to let you, either." I was very upset.

Suddenly my dream turned around and we were living in a lodge in the same area. All the family was there and huge bull-dozers were up on top of the hill, working. We were given two days to move out or be buried under the rubble. We didn't believe them; but suddenly the earth shook and everything started falling around us. Then they gave us fifteen minutes to go. We were frantically searching through the rubble for clothes, shoes and the key to the car that was also buried. Only Gordon was in no panic, slowly gathering things, while I kept shouting , "Only five more minutes!"

I woke up still shouting, "Only five more minutes!"

Space Flight

I dreamed I was speeding through the universe in a little open-cockpit spacecraft that had translucent eagle wings, larger than the vessel itself. The body of the craft was a deep red color, and on both sides the word Cybercraft flashed on and off in silver florescent letters. As I sat there, captivated by the splendor of the twinkling galaxies, I had no real sense of movement at all. The stars and planets seemed to be approaching my way, looming large and imposing in glorious shades of color, then slowly receding out of sight behind me. Every few minutes a shooting star went zooming by me, so close I could almost reach out and touch it. The sight of all this celestial beauty filled me with an indescribable ecstasy. I wanted to stay up there forever.

Somehow, though, I knew we were traveling at the speed of light, and I seemed to be on some kind of important mission that would be revealed when I reached my destination...wherever that would be.

"Whatever is powering this craft?" I asked myself in wonderment. And a million voices answered in unison.

"Thought waves...thought waves," they cried, "You are our first experiment in space! Just look what we can do! We're in the process of gathering all the stars and planets in the universe into our web!"

(Dedicated to Reloj, who said, "We will one day own the net...")

My Bus Ride

I was on a huge overcrowded bus on the way home from an extended trip somewhere. The road was very rough, and we were being jostled along, bumping into one another. Everyone had suitcases or heavy backpacks, and they seemed to be in good spirits. Everyone but me, because it was a huge city and I couldn't get up to the driver's seat to point out my destination. I had lost my voice for some reason and couldn't speak.

We kept stopping and letting people out, but more would take their places all loaded down with luggage. I was squeezed in too tightly to move. The driver kept going on his route; every once in a long while passing by the house where my family was waiting for me. I finally resorted to entreating the folks on either side of me with wild gestures. They just watched me in sympathy. I could see concern on their faces and the pitying glances passed between them. The frustration I felt was becoming unbearable. At last I looked out the window and saw a familiar site ahead. I knew if I could just get off the bus, I could somehow manage to get "home."

I tried to stand up and point it out to the driver, but my fellow passengers wouldn't let me. They kept pushing me down and consoling me, thinking that I was a mental case. It ended up with a massive struggle as I tried to leave that bus. I was kicking and screaming and pushing with all my might, and finally (thank God), I woke up in a big sweat.

The Invention

My daughter, Norma, and I decided to go for a walk. It was early spring, in the Yukon; the snow had just started to melt, leaving muddy puddles in the middle of the country path. The day was sunny and bright, and we trudged on and on, skirting our way around the potholes and trying to stay up on the frozen snow around the edges. After a while we found ourselves in surroundings we didn't recognize, so turned to go back.

This was not to be, however, as the return trail had changed, and all we saw ahead of us was a long hill, sloping up and up; with no tracks at all. Miles ahead, on the crest of the hill, almost out of sight, stood a building. We had to reach it before the darkness closed in on us, there was no doubt about that, so we began the long climb to the top grabbing at bushes along the way to keep our boots from slipping on the icy snow.

After what seemed like an eternity, we reached our destination, which turned out to be a large building with many rooms. At first we thought it was empty, but then the door opened and a child of about four years old stepped outside. His mother was behind him, and when she saw Norma and I, she jerked him back inside. About to close the door again; she must have noticed how tired we looked. Glancing furtively all around her, she put her finger over her mouth for silence and let us inside.

"They don't want any outsiders here," she said. "You'll have to go as soon as your clothes are dry." She led us into what seemed to be a motel room, and disappeared.

Suddenly, the room was full of people rushing around. Two

men wheeled in a big red box in on a trolley and reverently deposited it in the middle of the floor. Others arranged tools and paraphernalia on a large table. There was an air of great expectancy and excitement as they went about their various tasks. No one seemed to notice Norma and I sitting there in bewilderment. Finally, I could stand it no longer. I went up to one of the white-coated men, and asked, "Where are we, and what is going on?"

"Oh," he said, "this is a scientific research lab, and today we're testing a project we've been working on for many years. It's my own invention," he added modestly, but with obvious pride.

The hustle and bustle finally subsided, and everyone drew back in a big circle, around the huge red box, which was now all fitted up with tubes, cables and levers. We had to admit it was a truly inspiring work of technology, even though it was an unfamiliar sight to us.

The head technician stepped forward and made his announcement. "This, ladies and gentlemen, is the moment we've all been waiting for. Please stand back, and it may be prudent for you to put your hands over your ears, as we are not certain of the noise level, until it has been tested."

He then reached into one of the boxes on the table, and brought out what looked like a white cigarette.

"But of course, it couldn't be that," I thought.

"All right, then, if you're all ready. The very first demonstration of our product."

He carefully put the little white cylinder into its holder, which protruded from the side of the box; he placed his right hand on a lever about a foot away, glanced over at the group waiting with quiet anticipation on their faces and pulled the lever...

It sounded like a canon going off. A tremendous explosion of air shook the room with a blast that knocked us all off our feet. As Norma and I picked ourselves up, dazed and shaken, the head technician strode to the far end of the room, reached down to pick something up and walked back to where the rest of the crew were now standing. Triumphantly he held out his arm and slowly opened his hand. There, in his palm, lay the crushed remains of a cigarette.

"Folks," he said, "I think we can honestly say that, due to the dedicated and sincere efforts of this group, the Cigarette Eradicator is definitely a success!"

The next thing I was aware of was slipping and sliding back down the mountain with Norma, both of us laughing so hard we couldn't have stood anyway, and when I woke up from the dream, I was still laughing out loud.

11

My Experience with Drugs

A long time ago I had to undergo a complete hysterectomy. When I regained consciousness after the surgery, the doctor left instructions that I was to be hooked up to an automatic morphine dispenser. For the first time I learned that such a thing existed. It sounded like a radical treatment to me, but the nurses explained that it was entirely safe and how lucky I was to have this apparatus. As I was in considerable pain, I soon learned to like this machine with the little rubber ball I could squeeze whenever I needed it. Apparently it's impossible to overdose on it.

About 10:30 p.m., the two nurses who were on night duty came in to make sure I was settled down for the night, and one of them said to me, "It's time for your pills, Mrs. Yardley."

"What pills are those?" I asked. "They're for your pain, and to help you sleep," she replied.

"But I don't have any pain."

"This will keep you from waking up; you can't give yourself morphine when you are sleeping, and the pain will wake you. Now, just give that bulb a couple of good squeezes, and you'll be fine."

Reluctantly, I let them talk me into taking the pills, pumped up the morphine and soon I drifted off to sleep. I don't know how long I slept, but sometime during the night a violent nightmare woke me up with a great start. I was soaking wet with perspiration, sitting upright (which I wasn't supposed to do) and far too disoriented to think of ringing the bell.

Where am I? I thought. A voice answered me, "I didn't say that!" But there was nobody in the room.

My head was pounding and my heart was thumping like a drum.

"I didn't say that!" said the voice again. It sounds just like me, I thought. Again and again my voice kept repeating, louder and louder, "I DIDN'T SAY THAT!" Frantically I looked around the hospital room. No one there but me. Finally I pinpointed the source of the voice. It was coming from the intravenous bag that was empty and flapping around above my head. My voice kept coming from it, repeating, repeating over and over again, "I didn't say that!"

I clamped my hand over my mouth. I had to be saying it, but I knew I wasn't. Certain now that I had gone over the edge to insanity, I tried to scream, but no sound came from my mouth. That loathsome intravenous bag just kept on in my exact voice, repeating, repeating, "I didn't say that!"

I clapped my hands over my ears. The last thing I remember was thrashing around in my bed, trying to escape that frightening voice. Mercifully, I guess I passed out.

I woke up to the sound of another frightened voice. The night nurse was shaking my shoulder, "Mrs. Yardley! You are not supposed to be in that position. Look at you; you're all curled up like a pretzel. And you've pulled the needle out of your hand; it's bleeding all over the sheet!"

She called in the other nurse, who grumbled because they were supposed to be going off shift now. "But we can't leave her for the morning shift, wouldn't want them to see her like this."

They got me straightened out and cleaned up, filled up the bag, which should never have been allowed to empty in the first place; and one of them handed me a little glass of water and three pills. They seemed in a great hurry to leave.

I was still hooked up to the morphine pump, but even though I was groggy and in major pain, I didn't use it. When I saw the pills she was offering me, I could not believe my eyes.

"I don't want any pills!" I yelled at her. Something in my eyes must have told her I meant it, because she turned and both nurses left the room. Just as they were going out the door I heard one of them say, "Bitch!"

The doctor arrived on his morning rounds. "You're not looking very chipper this morning," he said. I explained to him what had happened during the night, and his face became very grave. In a tight voice he told me, "I'll be right back." He was gone for about fifteen minutes. When he came back, he explained to me that the Tylenol the nurses had given me contained codeine and that even though I had no record of any allergies, the combination of that plus the morphine had apparently caused my distress and hallucinations of the previous night. The nurses had seen fit to medicate me without any orders from him to do so. He was not pleased and neither was I.

I never saw either of those nurses again during my weeklong stay in the hospital, and I never heard my voice coming from the intravenous bag any more. Thank goodness!

After my husband Gordon passed away on December 20, 2000, I felt many things. Relief for him, he never enjoyed his leisure years due to health problems, and an aching emptiness that I thought would never go away. At the memorial service, our granddaughter Tanja, wrote a poem that expressed her feelings in a very touching way and articulated what the rest of the family held in our hearts.

To Grandpa

Our lives were meant to intertwine
Your large hands gently cradling mine
Through life's adventures, triumphs, fears
You were there to hug, to dry my tears.
To be my friend, to be my teacher
To respect all folks, and all God's creatures.
With an impish twinkle in your eye
You'd make us laugh, until we'd cry
With stories of the pioneers
And colorful friends throughout the years.
Though not a man of many words
Your actions said what was not heard.
Though time will pass, by heaven's grace

Your impact, time cannot erase
Nor dull the aching in my heart
For we were never meant to part.
A man of wisdom, pride and love
I know you're watching from above.
By Destiny's hand we'll meet again
And I will cherish you 'til then.

We held a celebration of life for him in Carcross, Yukon, and next day, according to his wishes, scattered the ashes in Tagish Lake, where he fished commercially for the SS *Tutshi* in the late 1940s. Here is a poem that I wrote later.

Earth Chains

I used to feel like a butterfly,
Fluttering and straining at invisible chains
That held me—a prisoner to you.
Again and again I'd soar, skyward bound,
Only to feel the pull...the tug, tug,
That would bring me, limp and wilting,
To light on your shoulder once more.
Safe again, but still yearning
For heights unknown,
And places unseen.
If it wasn't for you, my heart would cry,
Just like an eagle, I'd take to the sky.
But youth fades away; the struggle goes on.
It's almost a year now since you have been gone.
The freedom I longed for
Belongs now to you.
Fly, fly my darling, my heart sings for you.
Just once in a while
From the heights you have found
Think of me here,
Still chained to the ground.

12

The End of an Era and Beginning of a New One

I sit here in the den today typing away at my computer and periodically glancing out the window at the small birds chattering away on the patio. If I raise my eyes slightly, I can see a row of cars and trucks driving along a ramp to board the small B.C. ferry, the *Quinsam*. They will soon be leaving for the twenty-minute trip to Gabriola Island. It is a beautiful sunshiny day in January. A small plane is taking off, and there is the usual activity out there in the water: sailboats, a tug and the Duke Point ferry just coming in sight around the point on its way to the Lower Mainland. Right now, because it is such a clear day (a bit unusual for this time of the year) the snow is glistening on the mountaintops way over on the mainland. After dark, I should be able to see the lights of three ski hills there. Every day I thank my lucky stars that I live on Vancouver Island.

Fred Horn and I will be celebrating our third wedding anniversary on December 17, 2005. It has been a memorable and exciting almost-three years.

Both of us had been living alone for a long time, before discovering that we shared many common interests. For ten years we had seen each other once a month at the computer club meetings, and occasionally our paths had crossed at the Port Theatre when a symphony orchestra was featured. But I was quite surprised when he called me one day, inviting me to go to a flute and guitar concert.

It wasn't very long until we were spending a lot of time together, coming to enjoy each other's company more and more. I think both of us had resigned ourselves to a single existence in our golden years; so it came as a bit of a surprise when we eventually fell head over heels in love! This wasn't supposed to happen at our time of life. I was a great-grandmother, for heaven's sake! (Even though, I'll modestly admit, I don't look, feel or act like the stereotype.) Fred is a year older than me and is still leading groups of canoeists and kayakers on rugged trips around the various islands.

Although I had never met his wife, Roni, who had passed away a year previously and Fred had never met my husband, Gordon, we decided that Gordon and Roni would approve of our choices; it's even possible that they are up there somewhere giving us the "thumbs up." We both sold our homes. Luckily for us, a larger condo suite on Cameron Island, in the Gabriola Building, came up for sale just at that time.

One of the first things we embarked on, after the Herculean job of moving two households into one was somewhat complete, was a trip to Whitehorse. Fred had been to the Yukon once before, on a paddling trip to Dawson City. This time we drove the Alaska Highway, with many stops and side trips along the way. He showed me many parks and places I had never been to before. We picnicked, explored and had a wonderful time.

Last September, Fred and I decided to fly to England for a month. One reason I wanted to visit the UK again was to do research on my family history. I had been searching on the internet for any records on my grandfather and grandmother on Dad's side of the family. My Dad being Eric Edensor Coke Richards. Over a period of five years my sporadic delving into the maze of information available on the Richards and Gee families had not been very fruitful. I ended up with drawers full of printouts on hundreds of people with the right names, but wrong connections. This, I have learned, is the story of a great percentage of the searchers out there on the internet. We all seem to soldier on just the same, because every time a new piece of the puzzle is found, the appetite is whetted, and back we go into the fray with renewed energy. It can be very addictive.

On our flight to Heathrow, I spent hours watching a big-screen television on the wall panel that was about two feet away from our faces. After a while the brightness of it became almost blinding, and yet when I closed my eyes it still penetrated through the lids. I was forced to keep them open against my will. Everyone else on the plane seemed to be peacefully sleeping through it all, but I had taken some pills, which I was told would prevent jetlag when we landed. Finally the program changed from continuous stunt skiing on stark white snowscapes to a couple of movies, which were quite good. One was *Cool Hand Luke* with Paul Newman and George Kennedy, and the other was *Anger Management* with Jack Nicholson. I cried and sobbed in the first one and laughed hysterically in the second. After that "Mr. Bean" came on for a short skit, and he also seemed hilariously funny to me in my present condition. (In my own defense, it was one I had never seen before.)

All this time Fred was calmly reading or sleeping (he had wisely refused the earphones). By now, I was feeling quite tired, but then the bright scenes of skiers on snow-covered slopes started up again. This was around four o'clock in the morning our time, and the suffering continued. That huge TV screen just kept on flashing, while everyone slept but me. Finally, I beckoned to a flight attendant and whispered, "Why do they keep it on?" She just shook her head and said it was regulations, and she couldn't do anything about it. I stayed awake all night, and swore that on the return flight we would get a seat far away from that screen.

Toward morning I was awarded with a most beautiful sunrise in a perfectly clear sky. It was very soothing to the soul, and a little glimmer of hope and excitement began to emerge. It was like a brilliant red and orange arc along the curvature of the earth. I tried to show it to Fred, but he impatiently shook off my hand and went back to sleep. I couldn't fathom anyone not wanting to see such a sight, but I guess if you fly a lot, you get to see it regularly. So, while the whole world slept, it seemed to me, I watched this wonder of nature all by myself miles above the earth. It was a strange and exhilarating feeling.

Finally, we landed at Heathrow Airport. We claimed our luggage and boarded a shuttle bus to the Hogarth Hotel, in the Earl's Court area, where we had obtained reservations by e-mail before we left home. It was around 4:00 p.m. September 8, London time. We fell into bed and slept right through until six o'clock the next morning.

After breakfast, we took the "Underground" to Kew, and walked from the station to the Public Records Office, now part of the National Archives. We researched all that day and most of the next.

We visited Hampton Court, by Underground and train. Waiting at the railway station we saw scores of trains going by on many tracks to destinations all over southern England all passing in quick succession, or even at the same time. It was quite mind-boggling to see this activity for the first time. Crowds of people all standing with their bags, looking up at the moving signs that announced where the next train would be heading, loudspeakers announcing the same thing. Many trains just rocketed through, nonstop, at sixty miles an hour or more. My head was swimming by the time ours came and we quickly grabbed a seat so we wouldn't have to stand all the way.

Cardinal Wolsey originally built Hampton Court Palace. After he was dismissed by Henry VIII, the king took over the

Uncle John's memorial in Holyhead, Wales.

156

place and it has remained a royal palace ever since. It is truly magnificent in a beautiful location on the Thames. Many of the staterooms are fully furnished and there are scores of huge paintings. The royal chapel is very, very beautiful. The food preparation and storage areas feature lifelike operations or displays and there is a huge, intriguing model of how the huge state banquets were conducted back then. So much to see, so little time. After that we returned to the hotel and relaxed for a while.

The next day we walked to the science museum in Kensington. We took in an Imax movie, then explored the rest of the museum, or at least part of it.

In Nanaimo we are frequently reminded we are due for a "big one"—meaning an earthquake of 8 or more on the Richter scale. So we took in the earthquake displays with more than the usual attention. The museum had built a replica of a Japanese grocery store with shelves stocked, created on a well-concealed shaker table. So you could set the scene for an earthquake up to 5.0 on the scale, then step into the store and wait for it to happen. Now we have some idea of how it will feel if the real quake arrives here.

Finally, I got to meet some of Fred's family, and what nice people they are. Angela, his niece, is a part-time policewoman, in her early fifties, doing the beat with a partner on the streets, and part-time counselor and adviser for teenage kids. She is tall, fit and slender, with very short platinum hair. Looks great in her uniform. Her husband, Tony, is retired now, except for a stationery delivery job with a buddy two days a week. He is originally from Sri-Lanka, and he and Angie travel back to his home there every couple of years for holidays. Tony spent most of one day preparing the most delicious meal for us. His specialty is Indian food and he does a superb job. He uses the raw grated coconut and many exotic condiments (yummy!).

The next day was family time with Fred's brother, Ted (Angie's father), coming over to visit. Angie's younger brother, Colin, arrived as well. He drives taxi for a living in London. Then we rented a car and proceeded to drive 1,300 miles before getting back to their house on our way home. As much as possible, we kept off the main highways, preferring instead the country roads and leafy lanes between the villages.

Frederick Horn in family pew at Hernhill.

IN SACRED MEMORY OF
FREDERICK SIDNEY HORN
OF THIS PARISH
(ROYAL ARMY MEDICAL CORPS
WHO WAS KILLED IN ACTION OCTOBER 10ᵀᴴ 1917.
AT YPRES;
AGED 24.

Frederick Horn
Sept 13, 2003

I loved Kent. We drove through the old villages, Harbledown was one, where most of the buildings had been there in the twelfth and thirteenth centuries. The day ended in Canterbury, where Fred spent his high school years. We followed in the footsteps of Geoffrey Chaucer, past the Falstaff Inn, featured in his legendary *Canterbury Tales*. We visited the magnificent Canterbury Cathedral. We also visited the little old church that his family frequented many years ago. There was the pew with the Horn family name right above it. I took Fred's picture sitting there, below a plaque that is dedicated to his uncle; it read:

In Sacred Memory of Frederick Sidney Horn
Of this Parish
Royal Army Medical Corps
Who was Killed in Action on October 10th 1917
At Ypres
Age 24

It had been more than twenty years since Fred had been there. We drove on to Herne Bay, a harbor-waterfront resort area with hundreds of people on the beach; we watched the young (and not so young) people demonstrating their expertise with very new and modern versions of "sea-doos." There were many glistening and streamlined varieties of them, large and small, shooting over the water and careening around the bay at incredible speeds. It was quite a show.

On Monday, September 15, Fred surprised me with a mystery trip; I didn't know where we were going this day. Not being very good at maps and geography in general, I had no idea that we were close to the White Cliffs of Dover until we pulled into the harbor, and there it was! I had always loved the song ("There'll be bluebirds over..."), and I had seen pictures of the white cliffs, but in my mind it was at the other end of the world and much too far away for me to ever see! And there it was, in all its glory, with the castle on the hill and the big ships in the harbor. In the far, dim distance I could just make out the shoreline of France. That's probably the closest I'll ever come to France, but it still sent a little shiver up my spine to be able to actually look across the English Channel and see that shore. Of course, I had to take my shoes off and put my feet in the water. Fred took my picture, and I picked up a rock on the beach to bring home for luck. We walked along the waterfront, ate ice cream and watched the huge ferries coming and going.

The next day we were on our way to Wales. This was a first-time experience for both of us. We traveled over rolling wooded hills; huge open green fields with thousands of grazing sheep; rocky mountain country; and fascinating villages, some new and some very old. Most of the street signs are in Welsh language— impossible for visitors like us to read; although, in tourist areas many signs are in English, as well as Welsh.

While there, we had a lovely visit with Fred's cousin and her husband, and stayed two days with them. They're coming to visit us next September for Fred's birthday. We certainly have a warm appreciation for the first-class treatment we received on our trip to England and Wales.

The flight back home was very relaxing. The plane was only about one-third full, and triple seats were available where one could stretch out and sleep if so desired. I took advantage of that for a while, but it wasn't long before I was up and staring out the window again. It was daylight; the sky was crystal clear. I guess for that reason the pilot didn't have to travel at the usual high altitude, so the view was mesmerizing. Flying relatively low over the Northwest Territory I gazed down on the white frozen ice fields with very narrow open blue channels weaving crooked paths for hundreds of miles.

The other sight, which I'll never forget, happened hours later. Passing over the Rocky Mountains, the snow-capped peaks seemed so close, looming up directly beneath our plane. It took one's breath away to see all that majestic beauty from the air.

Now, I think we'll be content to stay home for a while, until spring, that is, when probably the wanderlust will raise its irrepressible head again.

Epilogue

My Brother Ted

In 1945 my family received the devastating news from the Royal
Canadian Air Force that my brother Ted, who was a rear air gunner in the RCAF, was presumed missing in action. He was twen-
ty-nine years old. Ted had a little girl, Sharon, who was three, and
a wife, Dolly.

To: Mr. E. Richards
From: R.C.A.F. Casualty Officer
Date: March 26, 1945
Mr. E.E.C. Richards,
848 Nootka Street,

Vancouver, B.C.

Dear Mr. Richards:

It is with deep regret that I must confirm our recent
telegram informing you that your son, Flight Sergeant Edward
Gordon Coke Richards, is reported missing on Active Service.

Advice has been received from the Royal Canadian Air
Force Casualties Officer, Overseas, that your son and the entire
crew of his aircraft failed to return to their base after taking off to
carry out air operations over Ludzkendorf, located twelve miles
south, south west of Halle, Germany, on the night of March 14th
and the early morning of March 15th, 1945.

The term "missing" is used only to indicate that his where-
abouts is not immediately known and does not necessarily mean
that your son has been killed or wounded. He may have landed in
enemy territory and might be a Prisoner of War; and should you
receive any card or letter from him please forward it at once to the

Royal Canadian Air Force Casualties Officer, Air Force Headquarters, Ottawa. Enquiries have been made through the International Red Cross Committee and all other appropriate sources and I wish to assure you that any further information received will be communicated to you immediately.

Attached is a list of the members of the Royal Canadian Air Force who were in the crew of the aircraft together with the names and addresses of their next-of-kin. Your son's name will not appear on the official casualty list for five weeks. You may, however, release to the Press or Radio the fact that he is reported missing but not disclosing the date, place or his unit.

Permit me to extend to you my heartfelt sympathy during this period of uncertainty and I join with you and the members of you family in the hope that better news will be forthcoming in the near future.

Yours sincerely,

E M Beat
R.C.A.F. Casualty Officer,
for Chief of the Air Staff.

My brother, Ted.

Ted and Dolly

And then came another telegram:

To: Mr. E. Richards
From: R.C.A.F. Casualty Officer
Date: September 18, 1945
Mr. E.E.C. Richards,
848 Nootka Street,
Vancouver, B.C.

Dear Mr. Richards:

It is with deep regret that, in view of the lapse of time and the absence of any further information concerning your son, Flight Sergeant Edward Gordon Coke Richards, since he was reported missing the Air Ministry Overseas now proposes to take action to presume his death for official purposes.

When presumption of death action has been completed, you will receive official notification by registered letter.

May I extend to you and the members of your family my sincere sympathy in this time of great anxiety.

Yours sincerely,

R.C.A.F. Casualty Officer,
For Chief of the Air Staff.

The story of my brother E. G. C. Richards, with all his poems, can be found on the Nanaimo Malaspina College website (http://web.mala.bc.ca) by scrolling down to his name under WW II entries.

I did a lot of research on my brother and found the following through the 49th Squadron in London who still hold annual reunions for their veterans. Actually, I am now a member (absentee) of their organization.

The following information is from the book *They Shall Grow Not Old* by Les Allison and Henry Hayward, pages 641 and 758. (The book says he is from Vancouver, B.C., but this is wrong. It should have been Whitehorse, Yukon. Mom and Dad lived in Vancouver at the time he was killed, but our whole family was raised in the Yukon.) There is also some information on his fellow crewmembers, including the one they called "Corky," the only survivor of that mission.

Richards, Edward Gordon Coke FS (AG) R252612

KIA March/15/45 #49 Squadron (Cave Canem) Target: Lutzkendorf Germany.

Please see Thompson R.F. for casualty list and flight detail.) F/S/ Air gunner Richards is buried in BWC Charlottenburg, Germany.

Thompson, Raymond Franklin F/O (BA) J27160 from Belleville, Ont.

KIA March 15/45 #49 Squadron (Cave Canem) Lancaster Aircraft #RF 153 missing from a night trip to Lutzkendorf, Germany.

F/S J N McPhee, F/O G.A. Robinson, and F/S E G Richards were also killed.

One Canadian, FS Corrigan was either an Evader or was taken POW. Two of the crew (not Canadian) missing, presumed killed.

Flying officer, Bomb Aimer Thompson is buried in BWC Charlottenburg, Germany.

[Author's note: It has now been established that Corrigan (Corky) turned up a couple of days later (unharmed). He was very popular with all the crewmembers. Apparently Corky had a motorcycle that he treasured, and while he was missing someone had taken it apart. Mysteriously, when he woke up the next morning after returning, he found his bike all reassembled and shining Source: Newsletter from the 49th Squadron.]

A mountain peak, Mount Richards, was named after my brother on June 22, 1973, as is noted in the book *Yukon Names and Places*, by Robert C. Coutts. (I never knew about this until I read the book in 1980. Since then, I have obtained a certificate through the office of the Commissioner of the Yukon. There was no ceremony that I know of.)

Here are poems that Flt. Sgt. Ted Richards R 252612 sent home to the family while he was away at war:

The Unknown Soldier

There's an unnamed grave in the battlefield,
Rising o'er Europe's mud.
There's an unmarked mound in the sodden ground
That's wet with a soldier's blood.
Though his life he gave and his soul's passed on
He has not died in vain.
Though the world has lost this soldier brave,
The Earth's the one to gain.
He may be yours and he may be mine,
This Mother's son who's gone;
But he died for a cause that was just and true,
And his deeds shall live on and on.
For in every war there's an unknown lad
That dies in the battle's heat;
And his grave is held as a symbol dear
Where the Gold Star Mothers meet.
Oh, Soldier, as we pass your tomb
We breathe a reverent prayer,
And send it up to Him on high,
For you are in His care.
Little did you ever think,
As you fought by your buddy's side,
That you'd represent for the Allied Force,
All the men who died.

White Angels

There's an army of women, dressed in white, amid the strife
    and gore
along the far-flung battlefields on distant fronts of war.
They're the wounded soldier's guardians and they fight
    war's awful curse,
For it's horror, death, and dying, that's the lot of a
    Red Cross nurse.
You'll know them by their uniforms; on their arm is a cross of red.
They're our precious angels of the war, with no halo round
    their head.
With bravery, grit and courage; they work in the heat or
    the cold,
And we'll never forget the lives they saved, for their hearts are
    purest gold.

Heavenly Wings

Fly, fly, oh glorious bird-man, brave conqueror of the air.
With your silver wings above the ground, you'll fly forever
    there.
We earthbound men are envious, for the earth's ties hold us fast.
But you shall fly forever with a glory that will last.
Up, up through the limitless blue, there to commune with God.
Up, up through the azure hue, far o'er the earthly sod.
Kin of the mighty eagle, "Through adversity to the stars."
Up where the birds are regal, ever upward and on toward Mars.
Fledglings with man-made wings, strong of hand and heart,
Hark to the song that your motor sings, as it carries you
    through the dark.
Souring above the earthly sphere, close to the stars so bright,
knowing that God is always near, watching throughout the
    night.
Rest, rest brave fallen bird-man, your last flight is complete.
With a flaming gun you feared no one, and you did not know
    defeat.
There's a place for you in heaven, in the hanger in the sky;
There's a squadron up there waiting, and it's up to you to fly.

Your Wings

Your wings are a symbol of bravery for the goal at last attained.
They are part of the compensation for the knowledge you have gained.
Just a bit of cloth on your tunic, pinned on at a Wings Parade;
Not much in the way of glory, but it shows that you've been paid.
Do you feel your chest expanding, as if to hold that weight?
It's a natural reaction—but those wings won't make you great.
For the inner man is the master; that hidden hand of fate.
When you're flying your course in the future, your inner soul is the mate.
Those wings are new, yet they're tried and true, and they'll stand a trial of fire.
So it's up to you in your Air Force blue; leave nothing to desire.
Cover them with glory; leave a trail around the world.
On every front where you have to hunt—make sure the flag's unfurled.
They are covered in tradition. Though our service isn't old,
We back them with our hearts and life, and treasure them like gold.
We'll help them live forever, we'll cover them with fame.
Around the world they'll know us; we'll honour the Air Force name.
Those wings we have as aircrew will never know defeat,
For they're worn by men who will not quit, until the job's complete.
Carry your wings, you deserve them. And prove to the world you've the right
To wear them high, in a cloudless sky; don't stop till you've won the fight.
The fight for right and freedom and the privilege of life.
The fight that lasts forever, against aggression, greed and strife.
Those wings that are pinned to your tunic are as useless as they're new;
If you cannot stand and be a man—so the rest is up to you.

Hark to the Sounds

Hark to the sound of the bugle;
hark to the distant drum.
Hear the beat of marching feet
of the soldiers as they come.
The first contingent is leaving;
they're on their way at last.
The crowds are loudly cheering them on
from the streets where they're amassed.
A mother is softly weeping
as she kisses her son good-bye.
There's a soldier holding his lovely bride;
And he's telling her not to cry.
There is sadness here and sorrow;
there are hearts and eyes aflame.
And yes, there's some rejoicing,
with shouts of wild acclaim.
The thundering rumble of the guns;
the whine of the shrapnel shell
is music to these hardy sons
who fight in that bloody hell.
The sharp commands; the danger;
the crack of a rifle shot—
There go the sons of soldiers
Who have already fought.

Baby Sharon

I have seen the laughter shine in your baby eyes;
I have held your tiny hands, and heard your first faint cries.
I have known the dear delight of watching day by day
the progress of your stumbling steps, but now I'm far away.
I am not there to see you grow, that happy time has passed.
A stranger I shall be to you, when I come home at last.
But it is worth the sacrifice and all the agony
to know that you will live in peace, and be forever free.
    Your Dad,
    Ted Richards

The Sentry

I'm stuck with sentry duty, in the still of the winter night,
And I think of my buddies, safe in their bed
After the long days fight.
I cannot take a little snooze, or smoke a cigarette,
I have to stay on duty, or C.B. is what I'll get.
Halt! Who goes there? (my god what an awful place)
I didn't get an answer, but I'm sure I saw a face.
It was white in the winter moonlight, and flashed by my vision
*   there.*
The sentry watch beside a graveyard
is enough to turn one's hair.
The ghosts of the men that lie there are walking again
*   tonight;*
And me with a loaded rifle—in a sweat of unholy fright.
Each grave is marked with a tombstone, a symbol of R.I.P.
And soon there'll be nothing but tombstones
as far as the eye can see.
The flowers will grow in every row where survivors bury
*   the dead.*
In years to come most everyone will see the white and red.
But here comes the watch to relieve me,
By God but I'm glad that's through.
There's nothing so dead as a sentry's job, when there's not a
*   thing to do.*

The Bombing Run

Turning in for the bombing run, the drift is 'two to the port.'
The bombing angle is given, and we settle down for the sport.
Five miles down is the target; a patch on the earth below.
The bombardier asks for the heading; the answer is 2-3-0.
Steady, steady, level off, steady, now take her left a bit.
The aimer knows his business, and he's sure of a perfect hit.
Steady old man, keep her steady—I know the air is rough.
The run is nearly over, the strain on the nerves is tough.
Bomb bay-doors are open, the target in the sight;
The PFF has flared it—like a beacon in the night.

Bombs away! Lets beat it. Jerry is in a spot;
Flak is bursting round us, and the air is too darn hot.
The night is black as death, and the trip back home is long;
But we pranged another target, so we lift our voice in song.
Our tour is nearly over—just one more "op" to do;
And then I guess they'll screen us: providing we come through.

[This was Ted's last poem.]

Your Gunner Wings

Half a wing, but an A.G. wing, a brand of a hand of steel
He's a man that's there in the scorching air,
and no blow can make him reel.
There's a heart that's strong, for the battle's long,
and his eyes are clear and bright.
His aim is true, his errors few,
as he flies through the dark at night.
There's guts in a Gunner's make-up,
There's an urge to get out and fight.
There's a swagger there and a "devil may care,"
for he knows he's always right.
There's a gleam in his eyes as they search the skies,
A song of war in the dark.
There's a thundering roar in the muzzles boar
As the bullets find their mark.
His guns are his greatest treasure,
he knows them and trusts their aim.
They're the only way he has to pay,
or he can't stay in the game.
He's ready to face the rain of lead,
and he smiles when the slugs are hot.
The crew of the ship he flies with
Call him Johnny "on the spot."
That wing that you wear—be proud of it.
You belong there in the race.
And when the fighting is thickest,
keep a smile upon your face.
Wear it with all it's glory; a wing that you really deserve,
But whatever you do, be sure you're true
And show them you have the nerve.

The Soldier's Love

She's just a little French girl, I met over there in France,
Sweet, petite and cuddlesome; her name she said was Blanche.
I fell for her like a Howitzer shell, and I'm sure she fell for me,
But I told her that I had a wife and a little girl of three.
Now it's here today if we're lucky, and gone tomorrow if we're not;
The Lord looks after His own large flock, and some of the devil's lot.
So we had our fun together, the little French girl and I,
For I knew that my wife would understand that tomorrow I may die.
There's many a lonely soldier that's fighting far and near,
They sometimes need a woman to lend his heart some cheer.
Many a lonely husband with no intent to roam
seek solace in some woman for he misses his wife at home. '
So wives, don't judge too harshly, for man is just a man,
and he needs someone's companionship or life's not worth a
  damn.
So Blanche and I will be happy until this war is through;
And then, my dear, if you'll have me—I'll come back home to you.

War! War! War!

The dove of peace has fallen; her wings broken and bent.
The cruel, harsh cry of war! war! from every throat is rent.
A nation's sturdy youngsters are marching on to war:
A nation's sons and brothers are going towards death and gore;
You'll find their mangled bodies upon the battlefield;
And Death, the old grim reaper, will gather in the yield.
They'll give their lives for loved ones; for country, God and king;
So for these proud unfortunates, oh! let the vespers ring.
They're fighting for a worthy cause; they'll fight to their last
  breath;
And though they're heroes every one, the reward is mostly
  death.

Over the Top

The men in the trenches stood waiting; each minute seemed like
    a year
But the dawn in the East was breaking; and the time was
    drawing near.
Each man was impatient and nervous, like horses that champ at
    the bit:
And every one was iron-to-the-core, and all of them ready and
    fit.
Fit for the red heat of battle; fit to go over the top
To fling at the foe defiance; and fight till the moment they drop.
But there's the sound of the whistle; high and shrill in its blast;
Take one more look at your trenches, for that look may be your
    last.
So up and over and at them; an avenging wave of death;
You fight for a cause that is just and true, so fight to your dying
    breath.
And when you die in the battlefield, you have not died in vain.
The ones that come behind you will carry your banner again.
Charging across the wasteland, as a new day breaks in the sky,
You'll be driving the enemy backward; and they're leaving their
    dead as they fly.
Routing them out of the trenches; waking them out of their
    sleep;
Watching the lions of yesterday turning today into sheep.
Again we've tasted a victory; the drive went off as was planned.
And now we'll rest in the trenches of this newly conquered land.

— by Flt. Sgt. Edward Gordon Coke Richards
Remembered by His Family and Friends Forever